CIRCLE C MILESTO
ENRICHMENT GUIDE

Author: Susan K. Marlow

Enrichment guide created by Susan K. Marlow

(includes daily schedule)

CircleCAdventures.com

The Circle C Milestones books are
published by Kregel Publications.

Circle C Milestones Enrichment Guide
© 2020 by Susan K. Marlow

Study guide published by:
Circle C Creations
Tonasket, WA
www.CircleCAdventures.com

Thick as Thieves © 2015
Heartbreak Trail © 2015
The Last Ride © 2016
Courageous Love © 2017
by Susan K. Marlow

Books published by:
Kregel Publications
Grand Rapids, MI
www.kregel.com

ISBN: 978-0-9975067-3-0

Printed in the United States of America

Contents

Chapter activities include comprehension questions and vocabulary, as well as the specific thematic topics listed in italics below.

3. The Last Ride

4. Courageous Love

5. Answer Keys

Circle C Milestones Enrichment Guide

Content

The Circle C Milestones novels and enrichment guide can be used as literature curriculum. The activities cover a wide range of historical and language arts-related topics:

- ❖ Vocabulary, reading comprehension, and critical thinking questions
- ❖ Geography and map skills: cattle drive route, railroad routes, the Tehachapi Mountains, world's fair locations, New York, the Sierra Nevada
- ❖ Historical topics relating to the 1880s: ranching, lice, cattle rustling, Palace Hotel, dime novels, transcontinental railroad, *La Quinceañera*, 1880s arithmetic, cattle drives, Kaweah Oak Preserve, camels in the Old West, the chuck wagon, Fort Tejon, Los Angeles, New York City, the Brooklyn Bridge, world's fairs, Frank and Jesse James, Jules Verne's works, wind pumps, barbed wire, Old West prisons, University of California-Berkeley, *Pilgrim's Progress*
- ❖ Writing skills: the five elements of a story: character sketches, setting, story problem, plot events, solution; create a dime novel
- ❖ Just for fun: Pandora's box, crossword puzzles, word search, web fun, Spanish, trick riding
- ❖ Bible-related activities: Scripture copy work, the "fall," giants in the land, Bible mini-posters
- ❖ Answer key for all four books

Suggestions for Pacing the Literature Study

Each book takes 21 days to complete.

The (optional) Circle C Milestones lapbook activities stretch that to 28 days per book. It is available in Ebook ($12) or Print ($24) at **CircleCAdventures.com** and covers all four books with unique learning activities not covered in this literature guide.

Assignments are scheduled by day rather than by week, so you can use either a four-day or a five-day school week.

The books are chronological, but they are also stand-alone stories and need not be read in order. Multiple students can begin with different books.

<u>Note</u>: You have permission to copy as many pages from this study guide as you desire for your home or classroom. Not for resale.

Enjoy the adventure!

Susan Marlow

Andi Carter

Daily Schedule for Book 1: Thick as Thieves

*indicates an optional activity found in the *Circle C Milestones* lapbook.
(Lapbook activities can be skipped or purchased at CircleCAdventures.com)

	Day 1	Day 2	Day 3	Day 4
Thick as Thieves	Chapters 1-2	Chapters 3-4	– – – –	– – – –
Literature Guide	Page 7 Page 9 #1-6	Page 9 # 7-13	Pages 10-11	* Lapbook activity for chapters 1-4
	Day 5	**Day 6**	**Day 7**	**Day 8**
Thick as Thieves	– – – – –	Chapters 5-6	Chapters 7-8	– – – –
Literature Guide	Pages 12-13	Page 14 #1-7	Page 14 #8-14	* Lapbook activity for chapters 5-8
	Day 9	**Day 10**	**Day 11**	**Day 12**
Thick as Thieves	– – – –	Chapters 9-10	Chapters 11-12	– – – – –
Literature Guide	Pages 15-19	Page 21 #1-6	Page 21 #7-9	* Lapbook activity for chapters 9-12
	Day 13	**Day 14**	**Day 15**	**Day 16**
Thick as Thieves	Chapter 13	Chapter 14	Chapters 15-16	– – – – –
Literature Guide	Pages 22-23	Page 24 #1-5	Pages 24 #6-11	* Lapbook activities (2) for chapters 13-16
	Day 17	**Day 18**	**Day 19**	**Day 20**
Thick as Thieves	Chapter 17	Chapter 18	Chapter 19	Chapter 20-21
Literature Guide	Pages 25-27	Page 28	Page 29 #1-5	Page 29 #6-11
	Day 21	**Day 22**	**Day 23**	**Day 24**
Thick as Thieves	– – – – –	– – – –	Chapters 22-23	Chapter 24
Literature Guide	* Lapbook activity for chapters 17-21	Pages 30-32	– – – – –	Page 33 #1-7
	Day 25	**Day 26**	**Day 27**	**Day 28**
Thick as Thieves	Chapters 25-26	– – – –	– – – –	– – – – –
Literature Guide	Page 33 # 8-11	Pages 34-35	Pages 36-37	* Lapbook activity for chapters 22-26

Story Synopsis: When *Thick as Thieves* opens, Andi Carter is going on fourteen and looks forward to her mare, Taffy, delivering her first foal. What should be a routine foaling goes awry, and even big brother Chad may not be able to save the day. Later, Andi meets a new cast of characters who disrupt her life in more ways than she could ever imagine. Macy Walker, a homeless, ill-bred girl, invades the classroom and drags Andi to the brink of death on a runaway horse. Worse, a string of cattle rustling breaks out in the valley . . . and then the thieves go after the ranchers' horses. Andi is unwillingly drawn into a shaky friendship with Macy, and together they hazard a dangerous journey and learn the true meaning of compassion and friendship.

The character quality/theme for *Thick as Thieves* is "friendship." In your best handwriting, copy 1 Peter 3:8 from page 5 in the book. Color, cut out the poster, and memorize this verse during your study.

FRIENDSHIP:

UNSELFISHLY GIVING SUPPORT AND EXPRESSING COMPASSION TO ANOTHER

Thick as Thieves: Chapters 1–4

Read the chapters and answer the questions.

CHAPTERS 1–2

1. What is the setting for *Thick as Thieves*? _____

2. Why is Andi upset when she learns two of her brothers are at the yearly Cattlemen's

   Association meeting? _____

   _____

3. Who agrees to come out to the barn to check on Taffy? _____

4. What would Andi prefer to read rather than write in a journal? _____

5. Why doesn't Andi hear her brothers return from the cattlemen's meeting?

       A. They return after Andi went up to bed.

       B. The rain on the barn roof drowns out other noises.

       C. Andi is sound asleep.

6. What does Andi wish she could wear? _____

CHAPTERS 3–4

7. What news does Chad give Andi that throws her into fear for Taffy's life?

   _____

8. Name the foals and give a physical description of each:

   _____

   _____

9. After the foaling, what does Chad want Andi to do? _____

   _____

10. What does Andi want to do? _____

11. Andi's friend Cory is known for his money-making schemes. She imagines Cory proposing a
    peep show to exhibit the twins, but he'd want his "commission" for suggesting it. What is a
    commission? _____

    _____

12. What is the ranch foreman, Sid, looking for on the twins? _____

13. There is only one "cloud on Andi's horizon," meaning one gloomy thought. What is it?

    _____

For each underlined word below, write the part of speech (**noun, verb,** or **adjective**) on the given line. Then choose the best definition for how the word is used in the sentence. (See example.)

1. Mother says a proper young lady regards her feelings as a <u>petticoat</u>. _____ NOUN _____

    A. overskirt   C. bloomers

    (B. slip)   D. dressing gown

2. Andi ran her hand along Taffy's swollen <u>flank</u> and tried to stay calm. _____

    A. side   C. chest

    B. rump   D. stomach

3. Andi had been too wrapped up <u>fretting</u> over Taffy to remember what she ate. _____

    A. laughing   C. worrying

    B. crying   D. calming

4. Justin had quietly taken over as Andi's <u>substitute</u> father. _____

    A. replacement   C. sympathetic

    B. long-term   D. indulgent

5. "It's <u>customary</u> for young ladies to record their thoughts in a journal." _____

    A. highly unusual   C. exceptional

    B. normal   D. unconventional

6. Chad bosses me; I <u>aggravate</u> him. _____

    A. tease   C. poke

    B. soothe   D. annoy

7. Chad ran his hands down the mare's <u>quivering</u> flank and spoke softly. _____

    A. trembling   C. throbbing

    B. sweating   D. bleeding

8. Chad was often <u>impulsive</u> and quick-tempered. _____

    A. cautious   C. hasty

    B. patient   D. irritated

9. "Live twins are scarce as hens' teeth," the old cowhand <u>quipped</u>. _____

    A. said angrily   C. shouted

    B. cried   D. joked

10. Taffy perked up at the <u>concoction</u> and worked her way through it. _____

    A. liquid   C. medicine

    B. mixture   D. brew

THICK AS THIEVES: CHARACTERIZATION

Characterization is the technique an author uses to acquaint readers with the story's characters—both their physical traits and their personalities. Since characters drive the story, it's important that the reader get to know them soon . . . and to like them (or not like them, as in the case of a story's antagonists).

An author can introduce the characters in different ways. One way is to simply tell readers: "Andrea Carter was very worried about her mare, Taffy." Telling works, but it's not as interesting as letting the reader learn about Andi and her family naturally, through dialogue, action, and the setting (Andi's surroundings).

1. In chapter 1, what does Andi do that *shows* she is worried about Taffy foaling? (pp. 8-9)

_____

_____

2. Instead of *telling* the reader what Andi looks like, the author shows Andi doing something to her hair. What is it? (p. 8) _____

3. From the action in #2, we learn that Andi has _____ (color), _____ (length) hair that she wears in a _____.

4. What hints from chapter 1 show you Andi is impatient (pages 8-10)?

_____

_____

5. Andi's brother Chad is a major character. There are many hints that point to his personality in the first three chapters. List two things you learn about Chad.

A. _____

_____

B. _____

_____

SNIPPETS FROM ANDI'S JOURNAL

This is one of my favorite Bible verses—
"The horse is prepared against the day of battle,
but safety is of the LORD." —Proverbs 21:31

THICK AS THIEVES: FOALING

For eleven months (plus or minus a month or more, because mares often don't follow the "rules"), Andi has eagerly awaited Taffy's first foal. Being a rancher's daughter and well acquainted with stallions, mares, and foals, Andi feels confident Taffy will sail through the birth. Andi knows the signs of the impending birth and is on the lookout for them. She also knows that while the foal triggers the birth, the mare can delay it if she's nervous or upset. Here are the signs that send Andi running to the house for several days in a row, irritating Melinda and making her brothers shake their heads and chuckle:

* Two weeks before foaling, Taffy's udder filled and looked shiny.

* A few days before the birth, the muscles around Taffy's back end relaxed, and a little milk dripped from Taffy's teats.

* A day or two later, Taffy's attitude changed. She became restless, ate a few bites, paced, and had a faraway look in her eyes.

* That same evening, Taffy's tail switched. She paced, pawed, and nosed her flank. She sweated and got up and down.

Surely Taffy was in labor! But the most predictable thing about mares—as Andi found out when Justin checked on Taffy—is that they are unpredictable.

During early labor, Taffy was comfortable between contractions. She ate and appeared in no distress. But once the bag of waters breaks, a mare is in active labor. This stage of labor is fast. Usually only ten to twenty minutes pass before the foal arrives. When Taffy's foal did not make an appearance right away, Andi knew it was time to get help. If the foal is not delivered after thirty minutes, the chances of it being born alive plunges.

FOALING TWINS

When Chad tells Andi that Taffy is carrying twin foals, her response is, *This can't be happening! It's all a horrible nightmare. I want to wake up right now in my own warm bed, with Taffy safe in her stall and one healthy foal beside her. Not two. Oh, please, God, not two!*

Andi is right to feel horrified. To a stockman, twin foals are never a blessing. There is a 90% chance the mare will lose them before she reaches full-term. Most of the time the twins die in the first weeks of pregnancy. In the 1800s, no one could tell if a mare was carrying twins or not. Modern veterinary medicine uses ultrasound in the early weeks to detect twins. If twins are discovered, the modern vet aborts one of them so the other foal can survive.

If twin foals do make it to full term, they often cause the mare more stress. She has to feed, protect, and teach two foals. In most cases, one twin is smaller (like Sunny). Due to the added stress of foaling twins, mares sometimes reject one of the foals, usually the runt.

Foaling Time Crossword Puzzle

Complete the crossword puzzle by referring to the foaling study guide on the previous page.

Created on TheTeachersCorner.net Crossword Maker

Across

5. a male horse
6. Sometimes, the mare rejects the _____.
7. _____ percent of twin foals die before before birth.
11. Today, an _____ can show twins early in the pregnancy.

Down

1. the mare's nipple
2. a foal should be born within _____ minutes after the water breaks.
3. length of a mare's pregnancy (in months)
4. a mare's foaling time is _____
8. a female horse
9. the part of the mare that fills with milk
10. a young horse under the age of one year

SCRIPTURE MEMORY

If you haven't started learning **1 Peter 3:8**, begin to do so. It is the Bible verse that complements the theme of friendship for *Thick as Thieves*.

Thick as Thieves: Chapters 5–8

Read the chapters and answer the questions.

CHAPTERS 5–6

1. Andi had a hurry-up attitude about getting a foal from Taffy. If the foals were born at the beginning of January, circle the month Sabastian would have visited Taffy (see the previous pages about foaling for a hint.):   January   February   March   April

2. Andi would like to be finished with school when she completes the eighth grade.
   However, the Carter children must attend school until they are _____ years old.

3. Andi's marks in arithmetic are fine, but her worse subject is _____.

4. What is Andi's punishment for letting her schoolwork slide so badly?

   _____

5. Andi panics when she sees the sentence she must "parse" (break down into parts of speech). Can you help Andi find the subject and verb? Underline the subject once. Underline the verb twice. (Hint: "Man" is *not* the subject.) *The stateliest building man can raise is the ivy's food at last.*

6. What does Cory do that embarrasses Andi? _____

7. What is the new student's full name? _____

CHAPTERS 7–8

8. What discovery about Macy makes the rest of the students gape in surprise?

   A. She has lice.   B. She can't read.   C. She lives in the back of the saloon.

9. Who teases Andi after school about "catching" Macy's stink? _____

10. Why has Andi been riding Taffy to and from school for the past few days?

    _____

11. The Carter brothers are sitting around the supper table discussing bad times on the ranch. What has happened to get Chad so upset?

    A. Cattle rustlers have hit the ranch.   B. There's been a fire.   C. Some cattle are sick.

12. How long ago was the family's last encounter with this problem? _____

13. What is the name of the future Mrs. Justin Carter? _____

14. Who joins Andi when she goes outside to spend time with her colts? _____

THICK AS THIEVES: VOCABULARY-SYNONYMS & ANTONYMS

Synonyms are words that have the same (or nearly the same) meaning as the original word; *antonyms* have the opposite meaning. Below each sentence are four words. Circle the correct synonym for each underlined word. One of the words is the antonym. Copy the antonym onto the blank line. (The first one has been done as an example.)

ANTONYM

1. Shasta looked at Andi with dark, <u>limpid</u> eyes.　　　　　　　　　opaque

   colored　(*clear*)　*bright*　*opaque*

2. Sunny seemed <u>aloof</u> and somewhat capricious.

   frightened　*unhappy*　*friendly*　*distant*

3. The cover showed a <u>lurid</u> picture of a "wild Indian"

   crouched over a helpless settler, tomahawk raised.

   shocking　*colorful*　*dull*　*black & white*

4. Andi glanced at Chad, who gave her a <u>sympathetic</u> look.

   teasing　*understanding*　*disagreeable*　*unfeeling*

5. Andi found herself back in the <u>stifling</u> classroom.

   airy　*unbearable*　*stuffy*　*noisy*

6 . "How often do they have to spell a useless word like

   '<u>pusillanimous</u>'?"　*angry*　*brave*　*fearful*　*sad*

7. Sunny seemed aloof and somewhat <u>capricious</u>.

   flighty　*mean-spirited*　*predictable*　*lazy*

8. At this <u>dire</u> pronouncement, Macy lost her fight and

   became sullen. *expected*　*awful*　*urgent*　*wonderful*

9. Macy glared at the <u>spellbound</u> pupils.

   nervous　*distracted*　*tired*　*captivated*

10. Mr. Foster slammed the roll book shut and smiled <u>wanly</u>.

    brightly　*weakly*　*tiredly*　*sadly*

11. Jack looked like a frightened little boy, all because of one

    bold and <u>impudent</u> girl. *ugly*　*mouthy*　*respectful*　*cute*

12. "If I sit next to her, I'd <u>swoon</u> for sure!" Virginia said.

    cry　*revive*　*become ill*　*faint*

SCHOOLWORK: ARE YOU SMARTER THAN AN 1880S EIGHTH-GRADER?

1 bushel = 8 gallons

Andi saw Cory's math problem on the blackboard and thought, *Easy!* How about you? Can you solve the problem? As long as you know the conversion between bushels and cubic feet, the problem is easy.

1 bushel = 1.2 cubic feet (volume).

A wagon box is 2 feet deep, 10 feet long, and 3 feet wide. How many bushels of wheat will it hold?

First, it is helpful to draw a picture of the volume we want to calculate. We want to know how many bushels of wheat will fill the wagon box to the right. (To help a 21st-century reader get an idea of how big a bushel is, a bushel basket holds 8 gallons.)

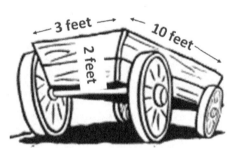

Step 1: find the volume of the wagon box.

(Volume = length x width x depth)

_____ x _____ x _____ = _____ cubic feet of wagon space.

Step 2: Divide the volume (from step 1) by the conversion factor of 1 bushel = 1.2 cubic feet to find out how many bushels the wagon bed will hold: _____ / (divided by) 1.2 = _____ bushels of wheat. (You may use a calculator. Andi did it in her head. Children in the 1800s were taught how to do mental math quickly and easily.)

- -

Are you ready for another arithmetic problem from an 1880s eighth-grade graduation test? (You may use a calculator. If you don't know how many pounds are in one ton, you will need to look that up somewhere.)

Find the cost of 6,720 pounds of coal at $6.00 per ton.

Step 1: Since the price needs to be per "ton," you need to find out how many tons 6,720 pounds of coal is. First, look up how many pounds are in 1 ton: _____

Step 2: Divide 6,720 by _____ pounds (in 1 ton) = _____ tons

Step 3: Once you know how many tons of coal you have, you can multiply it   by $6.00 per ton to find out how much you have to pay for your coal:

_____ tons x $6.00 = _____ (price for the coal)

A coal bucket

THICK AS THIEVES: TRAINING A FOAL

Some people (especially in the 1800s) began training—or breaking—horses when they were two years old or even older. This is where the "busting broncos" idea comes from. The rancher and his hands rounded up a wild herd of horses, confined them in a corral, and then—one by one—the cowboys lassoed their mounts and hung on. This was a quick (but often dangerous) way of "breaking" a horse to be ridden. Chad and his ranch hands use this method on wild stock, but they go about it differently with much of their "saddle" stock, like Taffy's new colts. Andi plans to train Shasta and Sunny from the time they are foaled. So, what will Andi do to train her colts?

SNIPPETS FROM ANDI'S JOURNAL

Chad helped me write a list of training tips so I wouldn't forget what to do. I copied it down in my journal and am keeping it out in the barn for easy reference. There's just one problem—how will I manage two lively foals?

<u>Newborn</u>: Let the foal get used to me, sniff me, and learn that I am his friend. Sit in the corner and watch. Rub the foal all over. If he doesn't like being rubbed in certain places, continue rubbing and talking softly. Since Taffy trusts me, Chad says this will work really well.

<u>A few days old:</u> I need to spend all of my time with the foal, watching him and holding him when he naps. Teach him right away who is the boss and how to stand still. Put an arm around his chest and another arm around his rump. Talk softly and hold him tight until he stands still. Then pat him and immediately let him go.

<u>One week old:</u> Put a halter on the foal for fifteen minutes at a time. Make sure each of the training sessions is short and fun.

<u>Two weeks old:</u> Teach the foal to lead with a halter and a lead rope. Use Taffy, since the foal will follow her. I'm going to use "walk on" to ask him to go. Never have a tug-of-war with the foal! Use a rope around his rump to make him go forward instead. As soon as he obeys, pat him and let him go. Teach the foal to stand tied. Brush and groom the foal every day.

<u>One to two months old:</u> Teach the foal the word "no." Be firm but gentle. Give him a sharp whack on the rump, if necessary, to teach him good manners. Ride Taffy, and the foal can come along. Following his dam will help the foal learn about creeks, flapping branches, and other frightening things. If Taffy is not afraid, the foal will not be afraid.

<u>Five or six months old:</u> Wean the foal away from Taffy

<u>One year old:</u> Teach the colt "walk," "stop," and "trot" on command. Start lunging the colt in a round pen, using a long rope while standing in the middle of the ring.

<u>Two to three years old</u>: train the colt to be ridden.

Foal-training Time Line

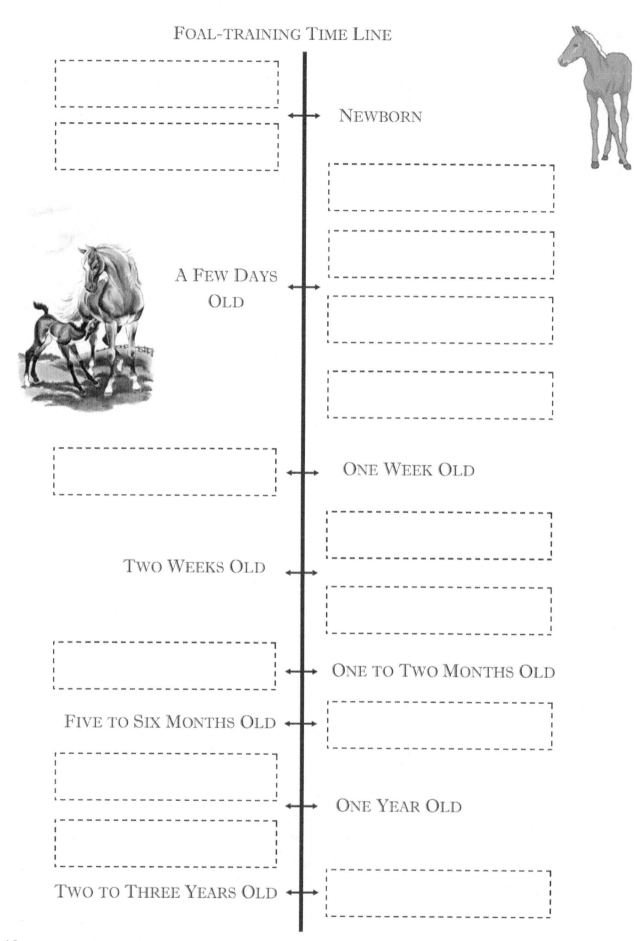

Newborn

A Few Days Old

One Week Old

Two Weeks Old

One to Two Months Old

Five to Six Months Old

One Year Old

Two to Three Years Old

FOAL-TRAINING TIMELINE

The previous page shows a timeline, with blanks for short notes on what training to do at certain ages. Cut out the foal-training instructions on this page and put them in order on the timeline.

Wean the foal away from his dam.	Rub the foal all over.
Sit in a corner and watch the foal.	Start lunging the colt in a round pen.
Teach the colt the word "no." Whack him on the rump if needed.	Teach the colt "walk," "stop," and "trot" on command.
Train the colt to be ridden.	Put a halter on the foal for fifteen minutes.
Teach the foal who is boss.	Put an arm around his chest and another arm around his rump.
Teach the colt to stand tied. Brush and groom him daily.	Teach the colt to stand still.
Spend all your time with the colt.	Teach the colt to lead with a halter and lead rope.

Thick as Thieves: Chapters 9–12

CHAPTERS 9–10

1. List the personality and physical traits of each of Andi's colts (see page 54):

SHASTA	SUNNY
_____	_____
_____	_____
_____	_____
_____	_____
_____	_____

2. Who is the young *vaquero* (cowboy) who wants to call on Rosa? _____

3. What does Andi hope Mr. Foster will agree to do for her?

    A. allow Andi to stay home   B. whip Macy into shape   C. give Andi a new seat

4. True or False: Andi's humble appeal touches Mr. Foster's heart and he honors her request.

5. What does Andi bring for Macy that shows she's willing to try to be friends?

_____

6. What keeps Andi's temper from spilling over when it looks like Macy might spit at her?

    A. She knows she will get expelled if she loses her temper.

    B. She's afraid Macy will punch her like she punched Cory.

    C. She wonders what her mother would do in a similar situation.

    D. She realizes the teacher is watching her.

CHAPTERS 11–12

7. Name two things Macy has done to stir up trouble in the schoolyard during recess.

_____

_____

8. What prompts Andi into taking action against Macy during the noon lunch hour?

_____

9. True or False: Andi agrees with her classmates that standing up was a good idea and now Macy will not give them any more trouble.

THICK AS THIEVES: VOCABULARY MATCHING

Match the underlined word in each phrase with the correct meaning. Page numbers where the word is first used are given so you can find the meaning using the context of the sentence. The first one has been done for you.

1. __D__ an old <u>adage</u> (p. 51)

2. _____ a <u>tirade</u> (p. 51)

3. _____ <u>petty</u> school problems (p. 52)

4. _____ to <u>harass</u> someone (p. 53)

5. _____ <u>brusque</u> manner (p. 56)

6. _____ to be <u>ridiculed</u> (p. 56)

7. _____ <u>savoring</u> the moment (p. 60)

8. _____ <u>loathsome</u> creatures (p. 64)

9. _____ a <u>farrier</u> (p. 69)

10. _____ a <u>skittish</u> horse (p. 69)

11. _____ to be <u>tranquil</u> (p. 78)

A. an abrupt or rough manner

B. minor; trivial

C. enjoying; delighting in

D. ~~a saying; a proverb~~

E. one who shoes horses

F. jumpy; nervous

G. an outburst; a rant

H. peaceful; calm

I. to be mocked or made fun of

J. to bother or pester someone

K. disgusting; revolting

DIGGING DEEPER

The relationship between Andi and her older sister is complicated, and often stormy. In chapter one, Melinda rolls her eyes at Andi's obsession about Taffy's wellbeing. However, in chapter 8, Melinda listens patiently to Andi's concerns about Macy and then gives good advice. Later in chapter 11, Melinda follows up to see how Andi is doing. Name a friend or family member with whom you have an up-and-down relationship: _____

Write about a time when you and this person got along wonderfully: _____

_____

_____

Now write about a time when you clashed and how you resolved it: _____

_____

_____

_____

_____

THICK AS THIEVES: LICE

SNIPPETS FROM ANDI'S JOURNAL

"Infestations" is Virginia's ladylike way of saying "lice." It scares me spitless to think Macy might really be harboring crawly critters in her tangles. My head itches just thinking about it. If I do catch them, I will simply die of shame!

Andi was right to be worried about picking up a lice infestation from Macy. Lice are very contagious, especially among children, who are often in close contact with each another. The tiny lice (singular "louse") live among human hairs and feed on tiny amounts of blood sucked from the scalp. Lice were not only an 1800s problem. Even today in the 21st century, they are a common problem. Lice are annoying and tough to get rid of. You can catch lice without even knowing it. Rich or poor, clean or dirty, a louse is no respecter of persons.

Lice are frustrating to deal with, but they aren't dangerous, nor do they spread disease. However, the bites can make a person's head itch, and scratching can lead to infection. The adult louse is smaller than a grain of rice and grayish white. The eggs (nits) are even smaller—like tan dots. After the louse hatches, it becomes a "nymph" (half-grown louse). In about ten days, the nymph is full grown. The old egg casings are easier to see than the lice. That's when you can tell if someone is infected. So, how does one get rid of these creepy crawlers?

If boys catch lice it's easy to get rid of them. Hair clippers and a "butch" haircut takes care of the problem. In the past, dousing a girl's hair with kerosene killed the live lice, but this treatment had to be repeated every few days to catch the new hatchlings. Sometimes, long hair was cut to make it easier to find the lice. Running a fine-toothed comb through wet hair every few days could also yank out the sticky nits. Nowadays, a doctor prescribes medicated, lice-killing shampoo. In addition to shampooing over and over again, the infected person's bedding must be washed in hot water. Brushes, combs, and hats must be checked and soaked in alcohol. Thankfully, lice don't survive very long away from the scalp.

Using kerosene (or any number of old-fashioned, "home" remedies) is *dangerous* and should never be used. Sadly, there are modern cases of children being badly burned using the "if it was good enough for great-grandma in the past, it's good enough for us" remedy of kerosene or gasoline. The fumes can ignite near a source of flame. And imagine the stink of   kerosene Andi and her friends would have to endure. No wonder she was worried!

JUST FOR FUN: A "LOUSY" POEM: Fill in the blanks with lice-related words that rhyme.

One _____, two _____. Finding them is not real _____.

A half-grown _____ was once a _____. If your head starts to itch,

you know you've been _____.

Thick as Thieves: Chapters 13–16

Read the chapters and answer the questions.

CHAPTERS 13–14

1. Andi's chapter 13 journal entry is full of plans to avoid Macy. Why does she add:

I think a journal can sometimes read like a work of fiction.

_____

_____

2. List two things you learn about Lucy Hawkins from reading chapter 13 (pages 80-81):

_____

_____

3. To the right is a picture of the Fresno County courthouse. What
   does Taffy try to do at Courthouse Park? _____

_____

4. When Andi takes off for town, she intends to give Macy what the
   girl deserves for her meanness. However, a Bible verse comes to
   her mind: *Be angry and sin not.* Think of an example of when it
   might be okay to feel angry (it is an emotion), yet it's not a sin:

Photo courtesy CA history &
genealogy room; Fresno Co. library

_____

_____

5. What does Andi do instead of lighting into Macy with both fists? _____

_____

CHAPTERS 15–16

6. Andi expects Mitch to get after her for being in the bad part of town. What happens instead?

_____

7. What does Mitch drop into Chad's hand? _____

8. What does Cory offer to do that makes Andi think boys are so silly? _____

_____

9. What are Macy's brothers' names? _____ _____ _____

10. Which brother interrupts Andi and Macy after school? _____

11. What does he want Macy to do? _____

_____

THICK AS THIEVES: SCRIPTURE MINI-POSTER

Oftentimes, Bible verses pop into Andi's head when she finds herself in a predicament. When Andi is faced with having to put up with Macy sitting beside her, she remembers Philippians 4:13, *I can do all things through Christ*. Ephesians 4:26, *Be angry and sin not*, comes to mind when Andi wants to pay Macy back for nearly killing her. Mitch reminds Andi that *God causes all things to work together for good* (Romans 8:28) when she thinks she should have ridden home with Lucy instead of riding Taffy. Later in the story, when Andi is really scared, Jesus' words from Matthew 28:20, *"Lo, I am with you always"* whisper in her mind and give her peace.

God has a way of using His Word to comfort His people and remind them how to behave in this world. The key is to memorize Scripture. God can't whisper His Word to you if you haven't "hidden it in your heart" (Psalm 119:11) in the first place. Look up the Bible verses listed above to see the full text (or choose a different verse to memorize) and neatly copy it on the mini-poster below. (You can make more copies of the page for more verses.) Keep the mini-poster in a handy place so you can look at it daily and memorize the verse.

THICK AS THIEVES: VOCABULARY-MEANING FROM CONTEXT

For each of the underlined words in the sentences below, write a definition in your own words. (See example.)

1. Perhaps I should <u>play hooky</u> from school for the rest of the term.

   "to play hooky" means . . . _____to skip out; not go_____

2. Maybe somebody would sweep Lucy off her feet while Justin was <u>dillydallying</u>.

   "dillydallying" means . . . _____

3. Justin getting married was as <u>inevitable</u> as the rising sun.

   "inevitable" means . . . _____

4. Andi could not find one <u>legitimate</u> reason for not liking Lucy Hawkins.

   "legitimate" means . . . _____

5. It was better to sit <u>mortified</u> in the dusty street than to be scared senseless.

   "mortified" means . . . _____

6. Andi hung onto Taffy's neck like a <u>leech</u>.

   "leech" means . . . _____

7. Andi looked for Macy near Fresno's most <u>frequented</u> saloons.

   "frequented" means . . . _____

8. If Mitch caught Andi near this den of <u>iniquity</u>, she would catch it for sure.

   "iniquity" means . . . _____

9. Why would he <u>goad</u> Macy into a fight and put her on public display?

   "goad" means . . . _____

10. Andi gave in and let Mitch <u>coddle</u> her a minute more.

    "coddle" means . . . _____

11. One or two of the Walker brothers were always <u>loafing</u> around town.

    "loafing" means . . . _____

12. "It sounds like they're determined to get themselves invited to a <u>necktie party</u>."

    "necktie party" means . . . _____

THICK AS THIEVES: SIMILES

A simile is a writing technique that compares things using "like," "as," or "than." For example, "The sun beat down on Andi's head *like a blacksmith's forge*." "Andi's legs *felt like jelly* when she stood up to recite." The similes compare the sun to a blacksmith's forge and Andi's legs to jelly. The first simile means it's very hot. The second simile means Andi's legs are weak and wobbly with nervousness. A number of similes are used in chapters 13-16.

1. Find the simile in the last paragraph on page 81 and write it here:

   _____

   _____

2. What is this simile comparing? _____

3. What does it mean? _____

4. Find the simile in the fourth paragraph on page 83 and write it here:

   _____

   _____

5. What is this simile comparing? _____

6. What does this simile mean? _____

7. Find the simile in the last paragraph on page 101.

   _____

   _____

8. What is this simile comparing? _____

9. What does this simile mean? _____

10. Copy 1 Peter 1:24 below. Circle the similes.

   _____

   _____

   _____

11. What does Peter mean when he compares people to grass and flowers?

   _____

12. Create some similes of your own by finishing these sentences:

   A. Macy caught on to reading faster than _____

   B. Standing up to the bully was like _____

   C. The school day passed slower than _____

   D. After grooming her, Taffy's coat shone as bright as _____

Thick as Thieves: Chapters 17–21

CHAPTERS 17–19

1. What causes Macy to sleep through the entire day of school? _____

   _____

2. When Macy sees the Circle C brand on Taffy's rump, she panics and says she has to leave.

   Why is she suddenly so jumpy? _____ Ⓒ

   _____

3. What makes Andi's feet slip out from under her and cause her to crash to the floor?

   A. She trips over all the junk on the floor.

   B. The floor is slippery from water and soap.

   C. She is shocked to see Macy's back and shoulders.

4. Macy asks, "Why would you bother with the likes of me? Especially when I've been so mean

   and spiteful?" Good question. What is Andi's answer? _____

   _____

5. Why has Macy slipped away and gone out to the barn?

   A. She has to get back before her brothers catch her away from town.

   B. She's planning to steal a horse.

   C. She wants to hide so she doesn't have to go back to her brothers.

CHAPTERS 20–21

6. Andi shrugs off her family's lack of response to her cheerful appeal for help with her

   colts. She thinks they're all just bone-tired from rustling concerns. What is the real reason

   everybody is so quiet at breakfast? _____

   _____

7. What promise does Andi try to get out of Chad? _____

8. Where have the rustlers stashed the Carter colts? _____

9. Knowing where her colts are being kept horrifies Andi. Why? _____

   _____

10. What has Andi done that makes her feel caught between a rock and a hard place?

    A. lied to Macy   B. promised to keep a dangerous secret   C. lied to her family

11. What does Andi pray for? _____

THICK AS THIEVES: VOCABULARY-MEANING FROM CONTEXT

For each underlined word below, circle the closest definition. Then use the word in a sentence of your own. (See example.)

1. Asleep, Macy looked young and vulnerable.

   invincible   (helpless)   sad   battered

   A newborn kitten is very vulnerable.

2. A swift reprimand always fell on a dozing student.

   scolding   accounting   justification   whacking

3. The colts nuzzled her and whinnied, imploring Andi to come in and play.

   hoping   telling   prodding   begging

4. Macy stood transfixed, staring at the two dozen young horses.

   stabbed   awe-struck   frightened   startled

5. "It's the most peculiar thing I ever saw," Andi said.

   prettiest   funniest   strangest   saddest

6. Andi quickly squelched that idea. Mother did not hold grudges.

   whispered   broadcast   skipped over   squashed

7. Macy might not know about guest etiquette.

   modesty   restraint   manners   routine

8. The whole day had turned into one colossal misery.

   gigantic   heart-wrenching   upside down   scary

9. Macy swept a wary glance around the yard.

   careless   happy   frightened   cautious

THICK AS THIEVES: CATTLE RUSTLING THEN AND NOW

Andi's family is embroiled in their worst nightmare—cattle rustling. How could rustlers get away with stealing so many cattle from the ranchers? For one thing, the rangeland covered thousands of square acres—too many to patrol with a couple dozen ranch hands on horseback. How did the rustlers go about nabbing somebody else's property? What did they do with the cattle once they had them in their grip?

Movies and TV often portray cattle rustlers as a couple of mischievous cowboys sneaking up on a herd of cattle and running off with a few head. True, there were small-scale operations, but most quickly developed into a large-scale industry. In the mid- to-late 1800s, cattle rustling gangs were stealing thousands of head at a time—and often killing the cowhands that got in their way. Many gangs worked together. One gang would steal a herd of cattle and sell it to another gang, who sold it to yet *another* gang—all of them making a nice profit along the way. With cattle changing hands so many times so quickly, it was hard for the law to track them down.

Gangs often sold rustled cows to "ghost ranchers," who were a little like Macy's brothers—they kept the cattle in remote places. Their herds grew fast, with no evidence of breeding or calving. Altering the ranchers' brands was a common practice among rustlers. Some rustlers even used a piece of heavy wire they could bend into any shape and carry around in their pockets.

Many cattle rustlers—if caught—met their fate at the hands of angry ranchers, who arranged a "necktie party." Hanging those guilty of rustling was illegal without a trial . . . but it was effective.

What about today? Has cattle rustling died out in these modern times? Not at all. As long as ranchers raise cattle and unscrupulous outlaws want them, cattle rustling will thrive. In fact, cattle rustling is worse now out West than it was in Andi's time. Just like back then, the cattle herd grazes miles away from the rancher's home—in the middle of remote rangeland. The cattle are counted twice a year—at calving and at selling time (like on the Circle C)—so it's hard to know if missing cows have died from lightning strikes, predators, disease, or have been stolen.

Rustlers stole cattle on horseback in 1880. Today they use a truck and trailer. They back it up to a small herd in the middle of the night and load up the cattle—with no one around to watch. Many cattle today are not branded. Some states don't even require it. A cattle seller needs only a bill of sale, which is easy to write up and show at the livestock sale. Some modern rustlers get away with hundreds of thousands of dollars of stolen beef. Cattle rustling in the 21st century is big business.

Cattle (and horse) rustling in the 19th century was a hanging offense. Today, the fine is $20,000 and twenty years in prison.

CATTLE RUSTLING THEN AND NOW

Using the study guide on the previous page and the Venn diagram below, compare and contrast cattle rustling in the 19th century with cattle rustling in the 21st century. List how the two are alike where the circles intersect.

WORD BANK

20 years in prison   hang rustlers   "ghost" riders   large industry $20,000 fine

change brands   fake bill of sale   trucks & trailers   on horseback   hard to track down

thousands of cattle stolen

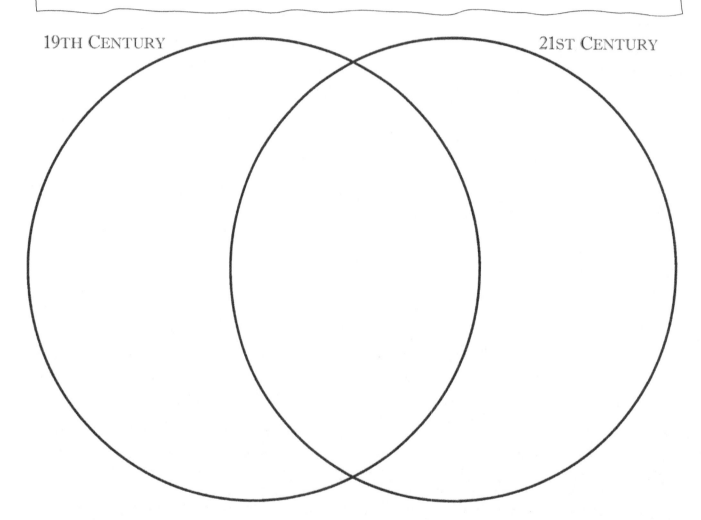

19TH CENTURY   21ST CENTURY

SNIPPETS FROM ANDI'S JOURNAL

Cattle rustlers are just like wasps. They sneak up and sting you when you least expect it, then they dart away before you can smash them. And just like a bee sting, the hurt doesn't go away. It just gets worse and worse. I guess I should be more patient with Justin, Chad, and Mitch, who are doing their best to clean out this nasty nest of cattle-rustling "wasps."

Thick as Thieves: Chapters 22–26

CHAPTERS 22–24

1. Why does Andi put her journal in full view just before she leaves the ranch?

_____

_____

2. "Straight ahead, the canyon's cliffs rose like sentries, marking the entrance." What two things is this simile comparing? _____ _____

3. What are "sentries"? _____

4. SETTING is where a scene takes place. It is often described using the senses of sight, sound, touch, smell, and taste. List some of the things Andi sees, hears, and smells on her way to (and once inside) Rock Canyon that contribute to her anxiety. For example, for the "TOUCH" sense, Andi feels the warm, July night as she's riding (see pp. 143–145).

SIGHTS	SOUNDS	SMELLS
_____	_____	_____
_____	_____	_____
_____	_____	_____
_____	_____	_____

5. Macy expects Andi to rescue Shasta and Sunny from the Walker brothers. What does Andi plan to do that Macy does *not* expect? _____

6. What prevents Andi from taking the rescued colts back to the ranch?

_____

7. How does Macy convince her brothers to spare Andi's life?

_____

CHAPTERS 25–26

8. What hard choice does Macy finally make when she helps Andi hide in the swamp?

_____

9. What has Macy brought along to protect themselves? _____

10. Who finds the girls in their hiding place? _____

11. How does Andi show her gratitude and her friendship with Macy at the end?

_____

THICK AS THIEVES: VOCABULARY CROSSWORD PUZZLE

Use the word box and the clues to solve the crossword puzzle vocabulary words from the chapters. (The first one has been done for you.)

ACROSS

4. ~~to shrink away; to cringe~~
5. to strengthen or support
8. something risky or dangerous
14. expensive, lush, or fancy
15. to be disbelieving; unconvinced
16. a guard
18. to be mixed with
19. a dilemma or predicament

DOWN

1. a lock of hair
2. churned; turned over
3. likely or possible
4. getting rid of; wiping away
5. rendered speechless with astonishment
9. making something look small
10. pressed close to her side
11. small hills; mounds
12. nagging; irritating
13. hidden; out of the way
16. a sofa or couch
17. swollen
20. gruesome; hideous

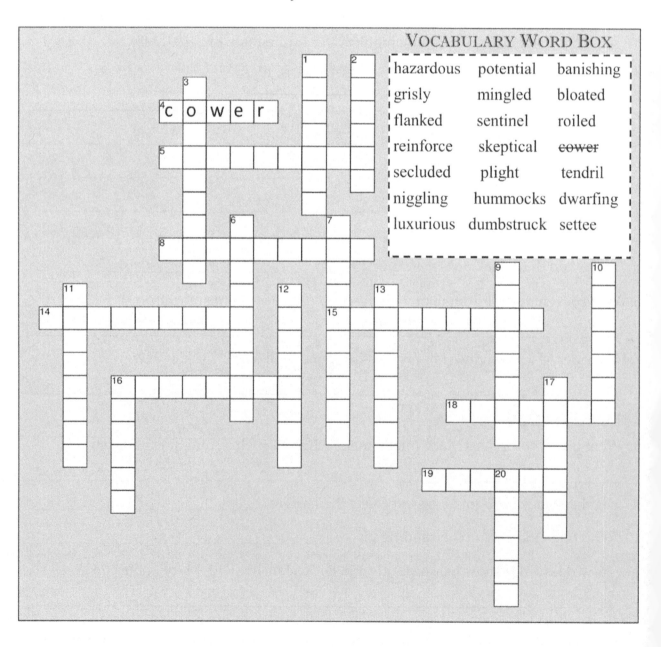

VOCABULARY WORD BOX

hazardous   potential   banishing
grisly   mingled   bloated
flanked   sentinel   roiled
reinforce   skeptical   ~~cower~~
secluded   plight   tendril
niggling   hummocks   dwarfing
luxurious   dumbstruck settee

THE PALACE HOTEL, SAN FRANCISCO

The wedding and reception for Andi's brother Justin and his bride, Lucy, take place at the Palace Hotel in San Francisco. The hotel was nearly new in 1882, having opened its doors on October 2, 1875. Seven stories high, it was the tallest building in San Francisco. With 755 guest rooms, it was the largest hotel on the West coast, and the most elegant. One rich man, Andrew Carnegie, remarked, "A palace truly! Where shall we find its equal? . . . The court of the Grand [Hotel] in Paris [France] is poor compared to this."

The Grand Court

Mr. Carnegie was correct. The Palace cost $5 million to build, and that was a *lot* of money in 1875. One of the astonishing features of the hotel was the skylight overlooking the Grand Court, where horse-drawn carriages delivered wealthy guests right inside the hotel. White-columned balconies surrounded the Grand Court, where guests could watch the comings and goings.

Palace Hotel

The Palace Hotel boasted four hydraulic elevators (called "rising rooms"), and each room had an electric call button to summon the hotel's staff. Rooms also had their own private bathrooms. The guest rooms could be joined together and opened up into suites for large groups (with a parlor that overlooked the street), or turned into long-term apartments for the many people who used the Palace as their permanent residence.

The hotel survived the initial damage from the great San Francisco earthquake of April 1906, but by late afternoon of that day, it had been consumed by the fires that followed the quake. Seven months after the earthquake, the "Baby Palace" rose, a modest, two-story structure. Then in 1909, the Palace Hotel was completely rebuilt from the ground up and took its place once again as the elegant, prestigious hotel it had once been. It still operates today.

SNIPPETS FROM ANDI'S JOURNAL

There's nothing like the Palace! Our suite was on the fourth floor. I could lean over the balcony and see the Grand Court below. It made me dizzy. And the elevator! It was a moving box that took me up and down on a cable so I didn't have to climb all those stairs. I went up and down the elevator once too often, and Mother scolded me. This is one place where I decided it might be best to act like a lady.

To help ease Andi's impatience with her recovery, Mitch generously lends her a stack of dime novels. Two weeks later, she's enjoying *Buckskin Sam, the Scalp Taker*. Other outrageous titles in her pile included *Ralph, the Slasher*, *Crack Skull Bob*, *A Trip to the Center of the Earth*, and *King of the Swordsmen*, along with Indian stories of captivity and warriors going on the warpath.

Dime novels were published by the thousands in the mid-to-late 1800s. Most people lived simple but busy lives, working hard from sunrise to sunset. There were no movies, internet, or TV. Entertainment revolved around the home and church. Rodeos and round-ups (with competitions and trick riding) were fun but limited to certain times of the year.

In 1860, the Beadle brothers published a small paper book called *Maleaska, the Indian Wife of the White Hunter*. It was an immediate hit, selling over 65,000 copies in the first few months. The Beadles named their cheap paperbacks "dime novels," and they cost only ten cents each. Their series eventually included 312 books. Soon, other publishers were getting in on these hot sellers.

Dime novels were similar to today's paperback novels, comic books, and TV episodes all rolled up into farfetched tales of heroes, adventure, and danger. Sound familiar? *Star Wars* comes to mind. Instead of battling aliens in outer space, dime-novel heroes fought Indians and pirates, found gold, and battled stagecoach robbers. Some went on incredible journeys inside the earth. Real-life men like Kit Carson became larger than life in dime novel stories.

SNIPPETS FROM ANDI'S JOURNAL

If Mr. Foster catches anybody with a dime novel, he yanks it away and tears it up in front of the entire class. Cory and Jack have lost many books that way. I keep the novels Mitch lends me far away from schoolmasters and preachers. They don't like them and don't think children should put such worthless ideas in their heads. Mitch says dime novels are all in good fun. Thankfully, Mother agrees.

Most everybody liked dime novels—from boys (and girls like Andi) to cowboys (like Mitch) to presidents (like Abraham Lincoln). There were, however, many people who did not like the books for the reasons expressed in Andi's journal entry above. Like today, there were probably some stories best left unread. However, the majority of them were good, clean fun and cheap entertainment for thousands of people. Later, the price was dropped to a nickel ("Half-dime novels") so the books would be easier for children to buy. Dime novels never lost their popularity. They turned into today's paperback novels, but they don't cost ten cents any longer!

A DIME NOVEL: *CALIFORNIA JOE, THE MYSTERIOUS PLAINSMAN*

An excerpt from *California Joe*, a newly published dime novel (1882) for Andi, from Beadle's Boys' Library of Sport, Story, and Adventure; Volume 3, #54. Summary: *The Strange Adventures of an Unknown Man, whose real identity, like that of the "Man of the Iron Mask," is still unsolved.*

CHAPTER I—THE FOREST PHANTOM

"Who was California Joe?"

Kind reader, that question I cannot answer more than can I the queries: "Who was the Man of the Iron Mask?"

But from the time he entered upon the eventful career of a border boy, when he was in his seventeenth year, I can write of him, and many a thrilling tale of his adventures can be told.

But go beyond that night when he first appeared to a wagon-train of emigrants and became their guide, and all is a mystery, as though a veil had been drawn between him and the years that had gone before, for of himself this strange man would never speak.

One night nearly half a century ago a [wagon] train, westward bound, was encamped just where the prairie met the woodland and hills. It consisted of a score of white-tilted wagons, drawn by oxen, half as many stoutly-built carryalls, to which were hitched serviceable horses, and the stock of the emigrants, comprising horses, cattle, sheep, and hogs.

Perhaps half a hundred souls were in the train, half of them being hardy, fearless men, and the remainder their wives and children, seeking homes in the border land.

When the camp had been pitched for the night, an hour before sunset—for the train traveled slowly, retarded as it was with their stock—a few of the younger men took their rifles for a stroll through the woodland above, hoping to knock over a few wild turkeys and squirrels for the evening meal. They were quite successful, and lured on by the sport, they penetrated the hills for a couple of miles and only thought of returning when the evening shadows warned them that night was at hand.

"Heaven above! Look there!"

The cry came from the lips of one of the party and all were thrilled with the sudden exclamation, which told of something more worthy of attention than a wild turkey or even a bear.

All glanced in the direction in which the one who had made some startling discovery was gazing, and every eye became riveted at once in a manner that proved the thrilling cry of their comrade had not been uncalled for. There, some hundred paces distant from where they stood, was what appeared to be a horse and rider. The animal was snow-white and stood as motionless as though carved from marble. The rider was dressed in deep black from boots to hat and sat silent and still. Even in the gathering gloom his face, seemingly very pale, was visible, and it was beardless. Across his lap lay a rifle, also seemingly painted black, and a belt of arms of the same somber hue was about his waist.

The horse was saddle and bridle-less and stood with head erect, gazing upon the party. This much all of the young immigrants saw. But who was this strange being and his ghost-like horse? *(Read the rest of the story on the Stanford University library's dime novel page):*

www-sul.stanford.edu/depts/dp/pennies/texts/ingraham2_toc.html#note

Daily Schedule for Book 2: Heartbreak Trail

*indicates an optional activity found in the *Circle C Milestones* lapbook.
(Lapbook activities can be skipped or purchased from CircleCAdventures.com)

	Day 1	Day 2	Day 3	Day 4
Heartbreak Trail	Chapters 1-2	Chapters 3-4	— — — —	— — — —
Literature Guide	Page 39 Page 41 #1-6	Page 41 #7-12	Pages 42-44	* Lapbook activity for chapters 1-4
	Day 5	**Day 6**	**Day 7**	**Day 8**
Heartbreak Trail	— — — —	Chapters 5-6	Chapters 7-8	— — — —
Literature Guide	Pages 45-46	Page 47 #1-6	Page 47 #7-10	Pages 48-50
	Day 9	**Day 10**	**Day 11**	**Day 12**
Heartbreak Trail	— — — —	— — — —	Chapters 9-10	Chapters 11-12
Literature Guide	* Lapbook activities (2) for chapters 5-8	Pages 51-52	Page 53 #1-7	Page 53 #8-13
	Day 13	**Day 14**	**Day 15**	**Day 16**
Heartbreak Trail	— — — —	— — — —	— — — —	Chapters 13-14
Literature Guide	Pages 54-56	Pages 57-59	* Lapbook activity for chapters 9-12	Page 60 #1-6
	Day 17	**Day 18**	**Day 19**	**Day 20**
Heartbreak Trail	Chapters 15-16	— — — —	— — — —	— — — —
Literature Guide	Page 60 #7-12	* Lapbook activity for chapters 13-16	Pages 61-62 (recipes tomorrow)	Pages 63-65￼Page 67
	Day 21	**Day 22**	**Day 23**	**Day 24**
Heartbreak Trail	Chapters 17-18	Chapters 19-20	— — — —	— — — —
Literature Guide	Page 68 #1-6	Page 68 #7-12	Pages 69-71	* Lapbook activity for chapters 17-20
	Day 25	**Day 26**	**Day 27**	**Day 28**
Heartbreak Trail	Chapters 21-23	Chapters 24-25	— — — —	— — — —
Literature Guide	Page 72 #1-6	Page 72 # 7-10	Pages 73-75	* Lapbook activity for chapters 21-25

Story Synopsis: *Heartbreak Trail* opens one year after the events in *Thick as Thieves*. For her all-important *quinceañera* celebration (fifteenth birthday), Andi asks permission to accompany her brothers on a cattle drive to Los Angeles. Together with her young nephew, Levi, who is staying on the ranch, Andi and the Circle C crew embark on an adventure like nothing Andi envisioned. She is unwittingly plunged into trail events much riskier than annoying mosquitoes and lack of sleep. When the worst happens, Andi's brother Mitch is left shorthanded with a herd of 1,000 balky steers to drive to market. Andi is ripped from her dull, "safe" position as Cook's helper and given charge of the horses. Already exhausted, Andi must dig deep inside herself to find the strength to finish what she started.

The character quality/theme for *Heartbreak Trail* is "endurance." In your best handwriting, copy Philippians 4:13 from page 5 in the book. Color, cut out the poster, and memorize this verse during your study.

ENDURANCE:

THE INWARD STRENGTH TO WITHSTAND HARDSHIP WITHOUT GIVING UP

Heartbreak Trail: Chapters 1–4

Read the chapters and answer the questions.

CHAPTERS 1–2

1. How old is Andi when *Heartbreak Trail* opens? _____

2. Andi is lost in thought while she waits for her nephew Levi to reappear from the gully.

   What is she daydreaming about ? _____

   _____

3. What does Andi do when she sees what is happening to Levi?

   A. She panics and then gallops to the branding fire to fetch help from her brothers.

   B. She yells and waves her arms to frighten the cow away from Levi.

   C. She uses Taffy to lasso the cow to make her stop.

4. What is the name of the man who comes along in time to see the cattle scattered and Levi and
   Andi on the ground? _____ What is his ranch job? _____

5. Andi thinks her friend Rosa is *loco* because . . .

   A. she wants to return to Mexico.   B. she's engaged to be married.   C. she wants a job in town.

6. What notion does Sid McCoy insist Andi "get out of her head"? _____

   _____

CHAPTERS 3–4

7. What surprise question comes up at the supper table?
   A. Mother asks Andi what she would like to do for her upcoming *quinceañera*.
   B. Melinda asks Andi if she is willing to go with her to Aunt Rebecca's.
   C. Chad asks Andi if she'd like to accompany him and Mitch on a cattle drive.

8. How do Mitch and Chad decide who will boss the upcoming trail drive?

   _____

9. What is a *remuda*? _____

10. A trail hand on a cattle drive who takes care of the *remuda* is called the . . .

   A. flank rider   B. point man   C. wrangler

11. What are the names of the two women Andi uses as examples to prove ladies can follow
    their dreams and still remain ladies?

    _____   _____

12. Which brother convinces their mother that Andi ought to be allowed to go along on the

    cattle drive? _____

HEARTBREAK TRAIL: ELEMENTS OF A FICTION STORY

Every dramatic fiction story must include these five essential writing elements:

CHARACTERS, SETTING, PROBLEM, PLOT EVENTS, and the SOLUTION.

For now, we will look at characters and setting.

CHARACTERS:

1. In the first 4 chapters, you meet a number of characters. List as many as you can find in these chapters and give their relationship to the main character, ANDREA CARTER:

_____   _____

_____   _____

_____   _____

_____   _____

SETTING: The setting of a fiction novel is considered the *time* and *place* of the story. (When and where does the story take place?)

2. TIME: The timeframe for *Heartbreak Trail* can be either inferred from the context or found at the beginning of the first chapter. What is the time period? _____

3. PLACE: This aspect of the setting can vary as a story progresses. In *Heartbreak Trail*, the setting covers a good portion of the San Joaquin Valley of California. Where specifically does the story open? _____

Sometimes it is fun to have a map to sort out all of the different settings in a story. The map on page 6 of *Heartbreak Trail* is a map of California in 1883. Although the route of the trail drive is the author's imagination, the rest of the map is as it really appeared in 1883.

4. Find a current map of California and compare it to the map on page 6 in the book. What two lakes do you see on the 1883 map that no longer exist in California today?

_____   _____

5. The blank map on the next page is intended to be used throughout this study. It will help you get a feeling for where some of the major plot events in *Heartbreak Trail* take place. For chapters 1-4, add the following to the map (refer to the map on page 6 of the book).

   - Fresno   - Color and label Tulare Lake   - Color the Pacific Ocean

   - San Joaquin River   - Draw a house or a rail fence for the Circle C ranch and label it.

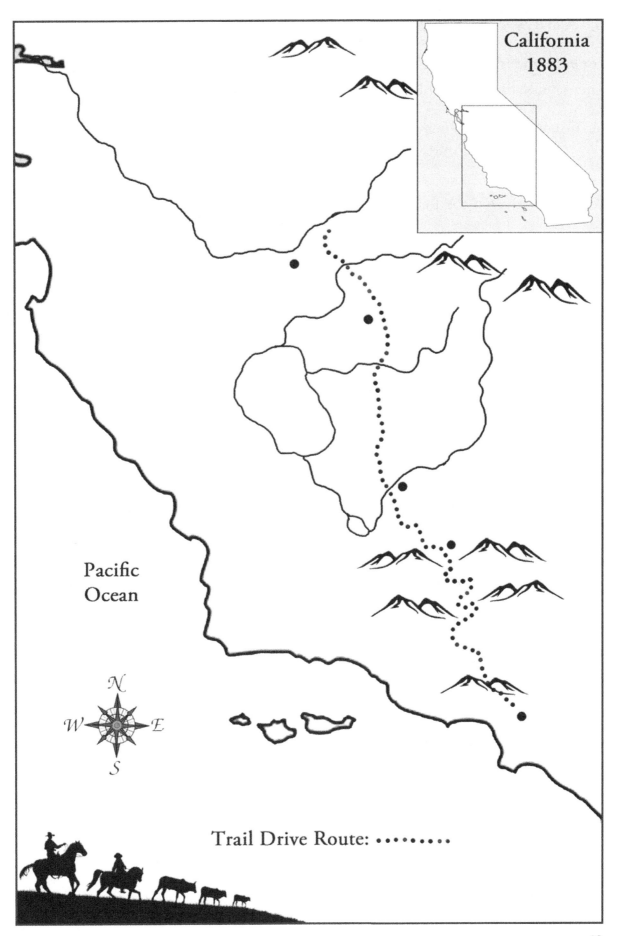

Pacific
Ocean

California
1883

Trail Drive Route: ●●●●●●●●●

For each underlined word below, write the part of speech (noun, verb, or adjective) on the line. Then choose the best definition for how the word is used in the sentence. (See example.)

1. The usual <u>jovial</u> foreman had turned prickly and short-tempered. _____ADJECTIVE_____

  A. sensitive   B. patient   (C. cheerful)   D. understanding

2. The men <u>pivoted</u> and took off. _____

  A. turned   B. saluted   C. agreed   D. yelled

3. Andi clamped her mouth shut and silently <u>stewed</u>. _____

  A. suffocated   B. fussed   C. laughed   D. mused

4. Up till now, Sid had been rambling. Now he was <u>meddling</u>. _____

  A. gossiping   B. comforting   C. helping   D. interfering

5. Levi <u>tittered</u>. Andi elbowed him into silence. _____

  A. grunted   B. whined   C. snickered   D. argued

6. Their Aunt Rebecca's reputation for <u>propriety</u> was well-known. _____

  A. respectability B. dishonesty   C. rudeness   D. bossiness

7. Mother's question had <u>piqued</u> the whole family's interest. _____

  A. bored   B. grabbed   C. repelled   D. put off

8. "Wouldn't *you* like to know?" Andi replied with a <u>saucy</u> grin. _____

  A. cautious   B. patient   C. hasty   D. sassy

9. "I think we need an attorney to <u>mediate</u> this dispute," Mother said. _____

  A. settle   B. stop   C. prolong   D. provoke

SNIPPETS FROM ANDI'S JOURNAL:

I love listening to Mother's olden-day tales. Afterward, she always looks at me like she shouldn't be too hard on me about not acting like a proper young lady. I'm thinking that maybe Mother wasn't such a lady back then either.

Heartbreak Trail: La Quinceañera (The Fifteen-Year-Old)

The Carters are Americans living in California, a state admitted to the Union in 1850 but still heavily influenced by Spanish colonization 100 years before. With so many ranch hands and neighbors of Latin descent (Spanish, Mexican, and native-born *Californios*), it is no surprise that the Carters have adopted the birthday tradition of the *quinceañera* coming-of-age for their daughters. The *quinceañera* celebrates the virtues of love, honor, and family—and recognizes the girl's journey from childhood to maturity. The custom highlights God, family, friends, music, food, and dancing.

The tradition of the *quinceañera* dates back to about 500 B.C and the time of the Aztecs. At fifteen, a girl became of marriageable age; fifteen-year-old boys became warriors. It was an important rite of passage. When the Spanish conquered the Aztecs in the New World, they blended their European customs with those of the native people groups. During 1700s colonial Mexico, young girls of the upper class were not allowed to dance in public before age fifteen. The *quinceañera* was their ticket into this aspect of adult social life, and the girls were eager to embrace it.

In colonial Mexico, wealth was a big part of a family's social status. It was important to throw a fancy party for their young daughter: an opulent, handmade gown, gold jewelry, and a lavish cake. This would ensure the family's chances of landing a good husband in the future.

In Europe, the rich also celebrated a young woman's "coming out," known as the debutante party (actually a full season, from April to July). The young women were "presented" with the hope that by the end of the season they would have found husbands.

The *quinceañera* went much deeper than the European model. The celebration was a time of affirming a girl's faith, family traditions, and her good morals. It was a time for welcoming a young lady into adulthood, but it was not a way of presenting her as eligible for marriage.

Today, the *quinceañera* remains a glorious and honored tradition among Hispanics around the world. Because many Hispanics are Catholics, their ceremonies include a very Catholic element to the occasion. The young lady receives a cross, a Bible or prayer book, and a rosary. After the religious ceremony, a reception is held in a hall or somewhere large to gather all the family and friends who have been invited. There is plenty of food, flowers, music, dancing, and a cake.

The "princess" of the day wears an elaborate ball gown and waltzes with her father and other members of her "court." At the reception, the guests toast the *quinceañera* and are invited to offer her their best wishes and congratulations.

Sometimes the custom of *The Last Doll* is included in the celebration. It can be used as a decoration or keepsake and represents that the girl is putting aside the things of childhood and will now focus on the things of a young lady. Sometimes she passes *The Last Doll* to a younger sibling to symbolize she is moving on.

The word search puzzle below hides twenty-three important words having to do with a young girl's *quinceañera*, both past and present. Can you find them? The words run vertically, horizontally, and diagonally. Have fun!

WORD BOX

Bible	cake	Catholic	dancing	faith	family	fifteen
flowers	food	friends	God	gold	gowns	honor
jewelry	love	music	party	prayer	princess	relatives
rosary	tradition					

SCRIPTURE MEMORY

If you don't already know this verse, begin to memorize **Philippians 4:13**, the Bible verse that complements the theme of endurance for *Heartbreak Trail*.

Heartbreak Trail: Chapters 5–8

CHAPTERS 5–6

1. Circle the words that describe the Carters' trail cook, "Cook":

    a gentle spirit • partially lame • a Mexican • appreciates help • old and proud •

    gruff • hard-working • a poor cook • feels sorry for Andi and Levi • bossy

2. How many cattle are the Carters driving to market? _____

3. Why has Mitch hired half a dozen outside, "temporary" trail hands for the drive?

    A. The cattle herd is larger than he expected.

    B. He doesn't want to empty the home ranch of all its cowhands.

    C. The new trail hands asked Mitch to hire them on.

4. Why does Andi want to get to know the flashy cowhand Toledo better? _____

    _____

5. Toledo's horse is named _____. What color is his glistening coat?

    _____ What color is his mane and tail? _____

6. Why is Andi alarmed when she hears the grandfather clock chime five times?

    _____

CHAPTERS 7–8

7. Andi thinks, *I need a little more of Flint's attitude.* What prompts this thought?

    _____

    _____

8. "The Serpent of Bear Lake" is the retelling of a real incident. Copy this link into your browser

    to read the story: **www.legendsofamerica.com/ut-bearlakemonster.html**

    What do you think the serpent really was? _____

    Do you think it is still there? _____ Why or why not? _____

    _____

9. What does Chad do to make up for scaring Andi so badly? _____

    _____

10. SETTING: Add the following locations to the map on page 9 of this guide:

    Kings River • Visalia • Draw and label the Kaweah River. It flows from the mountains,

    near to the town of Visalia, then dumps into Tulare Lake.

    How many days have passed? _____ How many miles have they gone so far? _____

HEARTBREAK TRAIL: VOCABULARY-MEANING FROM CONTEXT

For each underlined word below, circle the closest definition. Then use the word in a sentence of your own. (See example.)

1. "I want to get settled straightaway," Toledo told Mitch.

   sometime   immediately   later   soon

   You kids get your rooms cleaned up straightaway!

2. He climbed down, doffed his hat, and bowed low.

   removed   touched   lost   put on

   _____

3. "What's the ruckus?" Sid demanded to know.

   problem   story   commotion   answer

   _____

4. Hat in hand, the old man groused about Toledo.

   spoke praise   complained   whispered   yelled

   _____

5. "Bring me proof Toledo's a liability, and I'll send him packing," Mitch said.

   hindrance   fumbler   agitator   assistance

   _____

6. Chad and Mitch got an earful about that "strutting cockerel," Toledo.

   self-effacing   unassuming   frenzied   boasting

   _____

7. "I stayed behind," Mother said, "reveling in the adventure of the West."

   wallowing   working   delighting   cowering

   _____

8. Barely breathing, Andi listened, mesmerized.

   startled   alarmed   bored   captivated

   _____

9. The fun of a cattle drive had definitely waned.

   faded   grown   settled   expanded

   _____

HEARTBREAK TRAIL: HOW'S YOUR SPANISH? PART 1

Throughout *Heartbreak Trail*, you will come across various Spanish words and phrases. Most of these words and phrases revolve around the ranch's Mexican cook, "Cook" (his real name is Manuel). Chapters 1-4 introduce a few of these words, but in chapters 5-8 the Spanish really begins to roll from Cook's tongue, as well as from Luisa, the Circle C's housekeeper. The Spanish is presented in context so the words can be easily understood. Match the English translation of the following Spanish words and phrases. (See example.)

1. __D__ *No, chico, no necesito ayuda.* (p. 33)

2. _____ *Hay agua.* (p. 33)

3. _____ *¡Váyanse!* (p. 33)

4. _____ *Siéntate.* (p. 41)

5. _____ *Tómalo.* (p. 41)

6. _____ *comida* (p. 41)

7. _____ *Muchas gracias.* (p. 41)

8. _____ *Buenos días.* (p. 46)

9. _____ *¡Apúrate!* (p. 47)

A. food; meal

B. Go away; get going

C. Take it (eat it; drink it).

D. ~~No, boy, I don't need help.~~

E. Hurry up!

F. Many thanks.

G. There's water.

H. Sit down.

I. Good day; Good morning.

COWBOY SONGS

Cowboys sang to the cattle for a variety of reasons: singing helped pass the time while guarding cattle; it gave the cowboys something to do; but the most important reason was to keep the cattle from becoming startled at night. The darker it got, the more nervous the cows would get. Even the sudden slapping of reins or the *snap* of a striking match could spook the cattle and start a dreaded stampede. Cowboys were constantly on the move, circling the herd, singing, humming, or soft-talking the steers.

Many of the songs the trail hands sang became popular American songs of the West. To sample some of the songs that lulled restless cattle to sleep, you may want to type the song titles below into a search engine like Google. Some even have audio tracks to listen to. Note: For safety's sake, ask your parents before you search the Internet.

Get Along, Little Dogies   *The Streets of Laredo*   *Sweet Betsy from Pike*

The Old Chisholm Trail   *The Yellow Rose of Texas*   *Home on the Range*

Old Paint   *Red River Valley*

Everyone has a job to do on a trail drive. They follow a certain pattern when herding the cattle. Below are the jobs on the Circle C trail drive, along with the men initially assigned to the tasks. Read over the jobs. Based on the descriptions, fill in the jobs on the correct lines. Then, if you would like, color the picture. Note: There are more cattle on the drive than the picture shows.

Trail Boss (*Mitch*): keeps the records and gives the orders to the ramrod; rides in front.

Ramrod* (*Chad*): carries out the trail boss's orders and keeps the herd moving

Scout* (*Chad*): scouts half a day ahead for water, grazing, and stopping places

Trail Cook (*Cook*): drives the chuck wagon a mile or two ahead of the herd; cooks all meals

Point Riders: 2 (*Wyatt & Diego*): ride at the very front of the herd and lead the way

Swing Riders: 2 (*Tripp & Toledo*): ride near the front and make sure the herd turns correctly

Flank Riders: 2 (*Seth & Huey*): ride toward the back and keep the herd from spreading out

Drag Riders: 3 (*Joselito, Kirby, & Bryce*): ride at the rear of the herd and make sure the slow cattle keep moving; dirtiest job of the drive

Wrangler (*Flint*): in charge of the *remuda* (horses); usually one of the youngest riders.

* starred jobs are not shown on the picture.

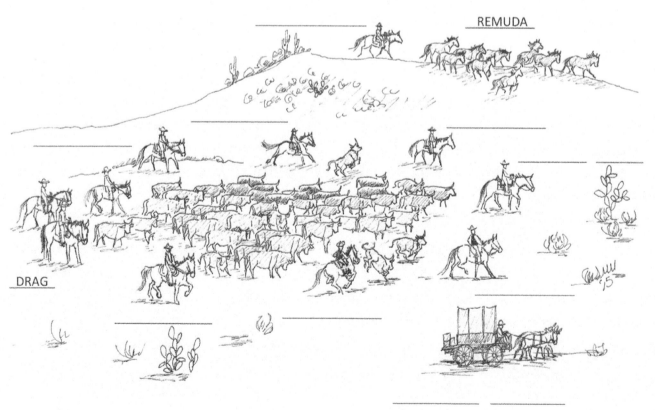

REMUDA

DRAG

The first cowgirls were rugged daughters of the frontier, who cut their first teeth chewing on leather harnesses. Most could ride and rope at an early age. While many girls learned the horse-trading business, they were also well educated for the times and could play the piano as easily as they could rope a steer. Most history books overlook the women who helped tame the West, resigning them to parlors and Ladies' Aid Society meetings. Amazingly, they were comfortable doing it all. Meet four of these daring girls:

Kitty Wilkins: I was born "Katherine" in 1857. Papa gave me my first horse when I was a small girl. He bought a sweet filly for two $20 gold pieces. My family moved all over the West and finally settled in Idaho. When I grew up, folks called me the "Horse Queen of Idaho." I rode the range alongside my hired hands, and my Diamond brand became known all over the country. The U.S. Cavalry bought my horses, as did Buffalo Bill's Wild West Show. I once took 3,000 horses to St. Louis and sold them myself. Then I changed clothes and entertained in an elegant fashion. Sadly, I never married. I was engaged to my foreman, but he was killed going after an intruder on the ranch.

Williams: I was a well-educated young lady. Father moved our family to Texas and established the Johnson Institute (of higher learning). I taught at the school (age 17), but after the Civil War, with all those loose cattle running free, I donned my sunbonnet, hired a few cowhands, and rounded up the strays to ship north. I became a wealthy young woman. In 1871 at the age of 28, I registered my own brand. Later, I became the first cattle queen of Texas. When I married Hezekiah Williams, I was able to secure a contract that kept all of my own property (unusual for the times). Hezekiah and I drove our herds together on the Chisholm Trail.

Prairie Rose Henderson: In 1908, I rode into Cheyenne, Wyoming, to enter a bronco-busting contest. "Sorry, no women are permitted to ride," I was told. As the daughter of a Wyoming rancher, I could ride just as well as any cowboy. I demanded to see the rules, where I found no official rule forbidding women to compete, so the officials were forced into allowing me to enter. The audience was stunned! I dashed out of the chute and . . . lost the contest. But I won the right for women to compete alongside men in rodeos. I was a showy cowgirl. I wore ostrich plumes over my bloomers and a blouse with bright sequins. I won many competitions but lost my life one winter during a blizzard.

Lucille, age 8

Lucille Mulhall: I was America's first true cowgirl (The term "cowgirl" was invented because of me.) At eight years old, I was already a skilled roper. By age ten I could lasso a running jackrabbit and rope a full-grown steer. Papa said I could keep any calf I could rope and brand, and I soon had a small herd that I marked with my belt buckle. I was never interested in dolls or tea parties, much preferring to train my ponies, lasso, and trick ride. When Mother sent me to finishing school a few years later, I returned before the year was up. I was born to be a "cowboy" and did not belong to that other world of fancy doings and fine accomplishments. I wore a split skirt and refused to ride sidesaddle. By the time I was sixteen, I could rope five horses all at once. In 1900 while still a teen, I weighed only ninety pounds, but I could break a bronc, lasso a wolf, and shoot a coyote at 500 yards. I performed at Wild West shows, where the crowds adored my antics (I loved those days!). I once put on a roping exhibition for the future president of the United States, Teddy Roosevelt. He said if I could rope a wolf, I could go to the inaugural parade in Washington, D.C. I brought Mr. Roosevelt his dead wolf at the end of a rope, and I went to the parade.

YOUR TURN

Choose one of these other daring women of the West to research. Find and print out a picture to paste in the box. Create a short biography in first person like the examples above. Write it on the lines below or on the computer and print it out.

HENRIETTA KING • LORENA TRICKEY • ANNIE OAKLEY • MARY ANN GOODNIGHT

Heartbreak Trail: Chapters 9–12

CHAPTERS 9–10

1. Why does Andi never want to forget the unwritten trail-drive rule "never go out to the herd alone at night"?

    A. because she was frightened half to death by night noises

    B. because she almost started a cattle stampede when she visited the herd

    C. because she was scolded for going out there alone with untrusted cowhands

    D. because she was supposed to be in bed, sleeping

2. Chad usually gets after Andi for doing something she shouldn't. This time, however, Mitch gets that privilege. Why? _____

3. What reason does Mitch give Andi for not wandering around in the middle of the night?

    A. Mitch doesn't trust the new hands. B. Andi could get lost. C. Andi might spook the cattle.

4. What is Levi in charge of each morning? _____

5. Andi is tasked with the job of _____

6. What "plague" of insects will not leave Andi alone? _____

7. True or False (circle one): Andi feels ill because she's coming down with the chicken pox.

CHAPTERS 11–12

8. Mitch is worried that Andi may have been taken sick with _____

9. Circle the reasons Cook believes Andi *está bien* (is fine):

    she's not throwing up • her eyes are clear and bright • she's not coughing or sneezing

    she has no fever • it is too soon to show signs of the disease • she gets right to work

10. One of Cook's trail-drive jobs includes doctoring sick men and animals. He has a fine supply of home remedies on hand. What tonic does Cook make Andi drink? _____
What is it supposed to cure? _____

11. What do Andi and Levi spy when they're chopping firewood in the brushy woods?

_____

12. When Toledo rides up, Andi is embarrassed to see him. Why is that? _____

_____

13. Young Bryce is a master campfire storyteller. First it was "The Serpent of Bear Lake."

    His latest tale involves _____ and the old Fort _____.

Heartbreak Trail: Vocabulary-Matching

Match the underlined word in each phrase with the correct meaning. Page numbers where the word is first used are given so you can find the meaning using the context of the sentence. The first one has been done for you.

Section A:

1. __D__ a cavalier attitude (p. 62)

2. _____ an inept Flint (p. 62)

3. _____ a "loose cannon" (p. 64)

4. _____ sick with the ague (p. 71)

5. _____ to reek to high heaven (p. 72)

6. _____ to reprimand a child (p. 74)

7. _____ to "hoof it" (p. 78)

8. _____ a monotonous trip (p. 80)

9. _____ to be "tetched in the head" (p. 81)

10. _____ a snipe hunt (p. 82)

11. _____ moseying around (p. 82)

A. to walk

B. a wild-goose chase

C. dull; tedious

D. ~~careless; casual~~

E. crazy

F. malaria; marsh fever

G. unstable; unpredictable

H. to scold

I. wandering; ambling

J. to stink

Digging Deeper

At the beginning of chapter 12, Andi's first instinct when she sees Toledo meeting up with two strangers is to hightail it back to the herd and tell her brother what he's up to. When Toledo explains and promises to tell Mitch himself, however, Andi decides she's being silly to worry. What is *your* impression of the charming but brash cowhand Toledo? Has Andi been fooled by his tricks and his beautiful horse? Or is Toledo a valuable member of the Carter trail-drive crew?

Toledo McGuire is (circle one) trustworthy • loyal • sneaky • pushy • kindhearted. Use clues about Toledo's character from the story (chapters 5-9 and 11-12) to support your impression.

_____

_____

_____

_____

_____

_____

THE KAWEAH OAKS PRESERVE

The Kaweah Oaks Preserve is the remains of the last riparian forest (woodlands along rivers) in California. It has been preserved so visitors can see what the now-dry valley looked like 200 years ago, before the settlers came. Today, the oak forest covers only 322 acres, but in Andi's day valley oak, sycamore, cottonwood, willows, blackberries, and wild grape covered *hundreds of square miles*, from the base of the Sierra Nevada range to the banks of Tulare Lake.

USING THE MAP ON PAGE 43 OF THIS GUIDE . . .

✓ Label the Tule River.
✓ Color all of the land between the Kings River and the Tule River light green. Label it "wetlands."

Early settlers called this land "The Swamp" because of frequent flooding and the high water table. The original people, the Yokut Indians, never made their homes in these wetlands but instead hunted, fished, and foraged for the wildlife and plant life they found here. The valley oaks in this area were also a source of the Yokuts' most important food—acorns.

An example of a Yokut hut made of tule reeds.

Abundant wildlife once thrived in these woodlands: <u>birds</u>—herons, hawks, owls, ducks, song birds, woodpeckers, crows, vultures, and quails; <u>mammals</u>—gray fox, bobcat, coyotes, rabbits, squirrels, raccoons, opossums, and skunks; as well as <u>insects</u>, <u>amphibians</u>, and <u>reptiles</u>.

By the mid-19th century, settlers were using this land mostly for cattle grazing, hunting, and wood-cutting. One family wanted to plant walnut trees in the area of the current preserve. Eventually, a dam was built in 1962, which put an end to the flooding, but the water table was too high to grow walnut trees successfully. Finally, the land was sold to a conservation group and has been kept just the way it was in the past.

If you have ever driven through the San Joaquin Valley around Visalia, you may find it hard to believe that this area was once teeming with water and wildlife. With a nickname like "The Swamp," it is easy to see why Andi was plagued by countless mosquitoes when she traveled through this wet, woodlands region.

HEARTBREAK TRAIL: ESCAPE THE WETLANDS

The Carters are taking their 1,000 head of cattle through the wetlands between the rivers just south of the Circle C ranch. It's spring, so the region has probably experienced some flooding in the recent weeks. Help the Carters' cattle escape the wetlands by following the maze through "high ground" around the area. Steer clear of the wildlife, especially coyotes and bobcats, animals that could startle the herd and cause a stampede.

This maze is sprinkled with a few examples of what you might see if you journeyed there in 1883, or if you visit the Kaweah Oaks Preserve today.

HEARTBREAK TRAIL: HOW'S YOUR SPANISH? PART 2

Are you ready for another Spanish lesson? This time you will write the Spanish words Cook uses when he talks to Andi. First, try to find the word from the box and write it on the line. If you can't guess the meaning, go back to the book pages and figure out the meaning from the context of the story. When you write your Spanish, don't forget to include the accent marks. Also, try to pronounce the words and phrases by reading the pronunciation guide.

```
SPANISH WORDS AND PRONUNCIATIONS
levántate chica (lay-váhn-ta-tay cheé-kah)  •  está bien (es-táh bee-én)  •  tómalo (tóe-mah-lo)
hombres (óhm-brays)  •  arriba (ah-rée-bah)  •  Qué pasa? (kay páhsa)  •  ven aquí (ben ah-kéy)
no importa (no impórta)  •  ándale (áhn-dah-lay)  •  Comprende? (cohm-prén-day)
Dónde está Levi? (Dóhn-day es-táh Levi)
```

1. (p. 66) Get up, girl! "_____." Cook nudged Andi.

2. (p. 66) Another nudge. Up! "_____. There is much work to do."

3. (p.67) Come here. "_____." Cook waved Andi over.

4. (p. 67) Cook furrowed his dark brow. "What's wrong?" _____

5. (p. 71) She's fine. "_____."

6. (p. 72) Drink it. "_____."

7. (p. 72). It's not important. "_____."

8. (p. 78) "Those two men _____ said they were just passing through."

9. (p. 79) Hurry! "_____."

10. (p.79) Where's Levi? "_____?"

11. (p. 79) "Never again will my wagon leave late, understand?" _____

REVIEW: Pronounce these Spanish words and write their meanings (see page 49 of this guide).

1. comida (coh-mé-da)_____

2. Muchas gracias (moó-chahs gráh-see-ahs)_____

3. Buenos días. (bwáy-nohs dée-ahs)_____

4. ¡Apúrate! (ah-pwúr-ah-tay) _____

5. No necesito ayuda. (no nes-say-sée-toe ah-yú-dah)_____

6. Hay agua. (I áh-gwah)_____

7. ¡Váyanse! (bý-en-say)_____

8. Siéntate. (see-én-ta-tay)_____

HEARTBREAK TRAIL: CAMELS OF THE OLD WEST

Bryce was not telling a tall tale about his story of camels packing supplies to Fort Tejon in 1858. It was true. No American ever took a camel seriously. They found it to be an ugly, bumpy creature with a face that shouted "stupid!" and eyes that popped out of its head. The camel was good only as a curiosity in a sideshow or a zoo. But all of that changed in 1848.

The United States had just won the Mexican War and taken over thousands of square miles in the Southwest (Colorado, Utah, Arizona, Nevada, and California). How would eager settlers move supplies across this untracked desert? Congress thought the camel would be perfect. After all, didn't camels do the majority of packing in North Africa? "Let's ship some camels to America and see how they work," the men decided. In 1855, Congress set aside money to do just that. They purchased thirty-three camels from Egypt and unloaded them at the port in Galveston, Texas.

 The army officers who worked with the camels made some amazing discoveries about this unusual animal. It could travel as fast as a horse but could carry much more weight than either a horse or a mule—about 1,000 pounds. The camel felt right at home in the American desert, even eating the bitter-tasting bushes that dotted the land. Better yet, when the camels were tried out in the Colorado and California high country, it was discovered they were fine in the cold and high altitude fine, and they were surefooted over steep slopes. They even swam the mountain streams.

By 1859, the government officials were "sold" on the camel. They wanted to bring 1,000 more to the Southwest. Unfortunately (or fortunately), the American Civil War of 1861-65 interrupted their ambitious plans. The camel might have overcome deserts, mountains, rivers, and heavy burdens, but it could not shake the worst obstacle of all: the animal itself.

Americans were used to their beautiful horses, not this ungainly, goose-necked beast with bumpy knees, a split upper lip, and a loose, sagging jaw. One settler insisted that the first time his horse saw a camel, the horse became so frightened "it climbed a tree" to get away.

Worse than its homely appearance, the camel's temperament exasperated the settlers. If a camel felt mistreated, it would spit a foul stream of saliva—and it was accurate up to ten feet away. Other times the camel sneezed a "mass of filth." When really angry, the beast kicked or bit the nearest person, horse, mule, or cow within range. The camel stank both in body and breath and could emit a long, piercing cry that rattled the ear drums from afar.

When the Civil War ended, American settlers were much more interested in using the new transcontinental railroad (1869) to transport their goods rather than either the horse or the camel. Some of the camels from this experiment were given to zoos. Others were set loose in the desert, where they were hunted by Indians or simply died off. The camel never found a permanent home in America.

Heartbreak Trail: Extra, Extra, Read All About It!

Write a front-page news story about the arrival of camels at Fort Tejon. Create a headline and then give the reader the exciting news about this experiment. Be as creative and interesting as you can. Make up examples from the soldiers' "eye-witness" accounts.

Use the five "W's" and "H" for article writing: WHO, WHAT, WHERE, WHEN, WHY, AND HOW.

Volume 1, Issue 1   August 10, 1859

The Fort Tejon Gazette

Heartbreak Trail: Chapters 13–16

CHAPTERS 13–14

1. After battling with herself the night before the river crossing, what important decision does Andi make the next morning? _____

_____

2. Label the following on the map on page 43 of this guide:

   • Kern River   • Bakersfield   • Buena Vista Lake   • an "X" at the river crossing

3. What has become Andi's favorite part of this cattle drive?

   A. eating the greasy, filling chuck-wagon food

   B. splashing through the innumerable valley creeks

   C. listening to campfire stories

4. Why can't Andi and Levi ford the Kern River on horseback as they have done before?

_____

5. What does Cook do in the middle of the river in spite of his bum leg? _____

_____

6. Circle the events that horrify Andi just after she and Levi survive the river crossing:

   the chuck wagon disappears underwater • Mitch narrowly misses being gored •

   the cattle stampede • a cowhand is trampled • the horses stir up the cattle

CHAPTERS 15–16

7. Andi helps Flint chase down the scattered *remuda* in the delta region south of

   Bakersfield. Draw cattails on the map on page 43 to show this marshland.

8. Why is Toldeo angry at Andi? _____

9. Mitch says Toledo is a "loose cannon." This saying originated during the days of sailing ships. During sea battles, the cannons were rigged tightly into a good firing position. Sometimes, though, the pitching sea could tear a cannon loose. A loose cannon was unpredictable and dangerous for the crew. Why does Mitch use this phrase with Toledo?

_____

10. When the river crossing is over, three people are missing or dead. Who are they?

_____   _____   _____

11. Andi has gone back and forth between sticking it out and asking to be sent home. As she searches for Chad, what does she decide to do? _____

12. What signal alerts Andi that Chad has been found? _____

60

Heartbreak Trail: Vocabulary-Meaning from Context

For each underlined word below, circle the closest definition for the context. Then use the word a sentence of your own. (See example.)

1. Chad's <u>ominous</u> words were meant for Cook's ear, but Andi listened.

   promising   helpless   (alarming)   uncertain

   The weather report for the next day sounded ominous.

2. Andi heard a *crack*, and the wagon <u>listed</u>, sending her and Levi over the side.

   tilted   toppled   broke in two   capsized

   _____

3. Gagging and <u>flailing</u>, Levi took a breath than disappeared under the current.

   paddling   thrashing   waving   begging

   _____

4. Andi forgot her own <u>fatigue</u> and squatted beside her nephew.

   worry   troubles   exhaustion   terror

   _____

5. Mitch rode hard and fast, close to a writhing mass of cattle gone <u>berserk</u>.

   wild   scared   disappeared   injured

   _____

6. Mitch would need every hand to help him <u>salvage</u> what livestock they could.

   tend   pick up   rescue   recover

   _____

7. Cook's <u>staunch</u> defense of all things proper soothed Andi's trembling spirit.

   unfaltering   loyal   indecisive   weak

   _____

8. Cook immediately <u>plied</u> them with heaping plates of hot food and gallons of coffee.

   pursued   supplied   frightened   hounded

   _____

9. Andi saw three riders <u>converging</u> on a copse of oaks.

   galloping   avoiding   coming together   looking

Before the chuck wagon was introduced, most cowboys ate "in the saddle" and relied on what they could pack in their saddlebags: corn fritters, dried beef, or stale biscuits. Cattleman Charles Goodnight knew the importance of providing his trail hands with plentiful, filling food. A cowboy could work longer and harder on a full stomach, and a trail drive could easily last two months (some lasted up to five months). If a cowboy knew there was good "chuck" (food) on the trail, he would be more likely to sign on to the drive.

Charles Goodnight got the brilliant idea of converting an old army supply wagon into a kitchen on wheels, complete with a rear-hinged door that lay flat to form a worktable. He added shelves and drawers so the cook would have everything he needed at arm's length.

The chuck wagon carried food and cooking gear, but it also carried other much-needed supplies: blacksmithing tools for horseshoeing, axes and saws to repair the wagon, sewing needles to repair clothes, first-aid supplies, bedrolls, and slickers, along with the crew's personal items. A cowboy on the trail needed a good night's sleep as well as good food, and the chuck wagon provided an opportunity for both by being the cowboy's supply station.

With so many things to cart around, Mr. Goodnight added heavier running gear (axles and wheels) to keep the chuck wagon moving over hundreds of miles of rough ground. This wagon design became so popular that the Studebaker company created and sold a special "Round Up" model in 1880. Many outfits supplied a large tent canopy that extended from the chuck wagon clear over the cooking area and to the campfire. It was propped up by wooden poles. Very handy during rainy spring days on the prairie.

"Cook" or "Cookie" managed the chuck wagon. He was an experienced person and second in command to the trail boss (along with the ramrod). He received $45 per month, while the other hands earned $25-$30 a month. Cookie was expected to serve as wagon fixer, doctor, referee in case of fights, barber, banker, and letter writer. While the cook was not expected to watch or guard cattle, he had a long day that started about 3 AM. He made sure coffee was available around the clock. He cooked a variety of meals in cast-iron skillets or Dutch ovens. He served plenty of beans, bacon, potatoes, biscuits, gravy, and the occasional son-of-a-gun beef stew (one of the steers).

Cookie found plenty of opportunities to liven up the menu with fresh eggs, milk, or vegetables if the trail boss authorized the trading of one of the steers along the way.

The next two pages show Cook's trail recipes. Cut out the recipe book, staple it together, and give the recipes a try. You can experience what Andi and the others ate on the cattle drive. Enjoy!

Cut out the booklet on this page and the next. Staple them together with the cover piece on top. Experiment with the foods Cook prepared on the trail drive. Have fun!

Cook's Trail Recipes

by Manuel "Cook"

SLAPJACKS

Note: Back in the 1800s, oftentimes no specific measurements were given. I have tried to substitute real measurements when I can to avoid a recipe from "flopping."

Flour: "some" (try 3 cups)

Sugar: "some" (try 1/4 cup)

Yeast: "a little" (2 teaspoons) **or** . . .

Sourdough: a cup (don't forget to replace and feed your sourdough!)

Water: enough to make a nice paste. Not too runny; not too dough-like.

Form into patties and fry in hot grease until brown. Be generous with the salt.

COOK'S QUICK DOUGHNUTS

- Put a kettle half full of fat over the heat.

- Sift together 4 cups flour, 1 cup of sugar, 1 teaspoon salt, 2 teaspoons of baking soda, and 1/2 teaspoon nutmeg.

- Beat 1/2 pound of butter until creamy and add to flour mixture.

- Beat the yolks of 2 eggs until creamy and add to flour mixture.

- Beat the egg whites until stiff and save.

- Add enough sour milk to make a soft dough; add the egg whites and mix.

- Roll out the dough, shape or twist, and fry the doughnuts in the hot fat (about 360°).

COOK'S EASY SOURDOUGH STARTER

When a trail cook found a good sourdough starter, he cherished it like a baby. Here is Cook's easy recipe:

2 cups of lukewarm potato water: make potato water by boiling 2 medium potatoes (cubed) until tender. You can eat the potatoes for supper. Keep the water.

2 cups white flour

1 tablespoon sugar

Mix the flour, potato water, and sugar into a smooth paste in a glass bowl. Cover and set in a warm place until the mixture doubles in size (a few days). You can remove some and feed with 1/2 cup flour and 1/3 cup water to freshen it.

When you use the starter, "feed" the rest as above. Store in a cool, dark place and use often. Or store in the refrigerator, but bring to room temperature before using.

TRAIL BEANS

Cook stored his beans dry then cooked them as needed. Here is an easy recipe with canned beans for modern cowpokes:

Mix together one 16-ounce can of each:

-pinto beans

-pork & beans

-red kidney beans

-black beans

-white northern beans

Cut up and fry 1 pound bacon, 1 chopped onion, and 1/2 garlic. Mix with beans.

Combine 1/2 teaspoon mustard, 1/2 cup vinegar, and 1 cup brown sugar. Simmer 15 minutes. Pour over bean mixture and bake over the fire in a Dutch oven (or you can use a crock pot).

SOURDOUGH BISCUITS

2 cups sourdough starter

1 or more cups flour

1 tablespoon sugar;

1 teaspoon baking soda

Combine all ingredients. If your starter is runny, you may need more flour. Knead the dough on a floury surface. Cut into biscuits. Bake in a Dutch oven until brown (or 375 degrees for 20 minutes in a modern oven)

FRIED APPLES IN BACON GREASE

4 apples (peeled or not) chopped

1/2 lb. bacon

Fry bacon, drain, and retain drippings. Fry apples in the hot bacon grease until soft. Combine with bacon if desired.

HEARTBREAK TRAIL: HOW'S YOUR SPANISH? PART 3

This time there are six new Spanish words and phrases to explore.

From the context of the story, write the English for the following Spanish words:

1. (p. 84) "It must be done," Cook muttered, "*pero no me gusta.*"

   _____

2. (p. 85) "*Silencio, chica,*" Cook broke in. _____

3. (p. 85) "I want you to drive the wagon ahead and find the best place for taking it across," Chad said. "Sí, señor," (Cook answered.) _____

4. (p. 89) "It is only a little debris from upriver. *No se preocupe.*" _____

5. (p. 96) "*¡Gracias a Diós!*" Cook shouted. "You and the boy were not drowned as I feared."

   _____

6. (p. 101) "*¡Basta ya!*" Cook growled, stepping between the two men. _____

DIGGING DEEPER CHAPTERS 13–16

1. After over a week of being on the trail, Andi discovers this cattle drive business is nothing like she imagined, full of mosquitoes, exhaustion, swamps, dust, and dirt. She almost admits she's had enough but then decides to stick it out. One reason is because she doesn't want Levi to finish something *she* cannot finish. What does this tell you about Andi's personality? List some character traits that come to mind that describe her.

   _____

   _____

2. What character traits describe you? _____

   _____

3. If you were in Andi's place, what would you decide to do and why? _____

   _____

4. Look up Galatians 6:9 and copy it. It's a good verse to know when you feel like giving up.

   _____

   _____

   _____

   _____

Heartbreak Trail: Chapters 17–20

Show how well you understand the story by answering the following questions:

 ## Chapters 17-18

1. Using the map on page 43 label: Tehachapi Mts. • Ft. Tejon • Draw a small stockade to indicate the fort.

2. When Andi learns Chad has been shot, her mind flashes back to what event two years ago?

_____

3. Mitch fires off instructions like a Gatling gun (p. 115). A Gatling gun was a rapid-fire, 1800s weapon and the forerunner of modern-day machine guns. This means Mitch is talking very _____.

4. Why is Andi so upset when Chad describes the men who shot him and stole   their beef?

_____

5. The trail drive crew experiences a loss of healthy workers. Why can't these men work?

Huey: _____ Chad: _____

Bryce: _____ Wyatt: _____

6. *Irony* is "the outcome of events contrary to what was expected." In the beginning of the story, Andi begged for a certain trail job. At the end of chapter 18, Mitch grants her wish, but she no longer wants the job. What job is it? _____

Chapters 19-20

7. Being shorthanded, Mitch shuffles the trail jobs around. What are these people's new jobs?

Andi: _____ Levi: _____

Flint: _____ Rico: _____

8. What good news does Andi discover about ugly Dusty? _____

_____

9. True or false (circle your answer): Andi discovers that being the horse wrangler is harder work than being Cook's helper.

10. Who confirms Bryce's tale about camels once being used at Fort Tejon? _____

11. Mitch sends Andi to ride drag. Whom does she see scuffling with Levi? _____

12. Andi makes a horrifying discovery about Toledo, the trail hand she once admired. What is it? _____

HEARTBREAK TRAIL: VOCABULARY: MEANING FROM CONTEXT

For each of the underlined words in the sentences below, write a definition in your own words.
Use an online dictionary for help if needed. (See example.)

1. "This was not an accident. I think Chad was <u>bushwhacked</u>, and not long ago."

   "bushwhacked" means . . . <u>attacked unexpectedly; ambushed</u>

2. Right then Andi knew she was going to <u>swoon</u> . . . just like a prissy girl.

   "swoon" means . . . _____

3. Andi looked up to see Mitch rein in his horse and <u>vault</u> out of the saddle.

   "vault" means . . . _____

4. Cook's loud <u>guffaw</u> confirmed that Andi had missed everything Mitch said.

   "guffaw" means . . . _____

5. Andi had been filled to the brim with energy and so <u>cocksure</u> of herself before the drive.

   "cocksure" means . . . _____

6. Signs of an <u>improvised</u> breakfast lay everywhere.

   "improvised" means . . . _____

7. The <u>enormity</u> of this new responsibility made Andi gulp.

   "enormity" means . . . _____

8. Toledo hinted that the current leadership could be blamed for yesterday's <u>calamity</u>.

   "calamity" means . . . _____

9. The drover reached around Andi and <u>hoisted</u> her saddle with one hand.

   "hoisted" means . . . _____

10. It was as if the <u>wily</u> steers knew a couple of greenhorns were in charge.

    "wily" means . . . _____

11. Mitch looked <u>haggard</u>, and more than a little frustrated.

    "haggard" means . . . _____

12. The shock of seeing the steers scattered and Levi hurt <u>befuddled</u> Andi.

    "befuddled" means . . . _____

13. Toledo seemed <u>impervious</u> to the pain.

    "impervious" means . . . _____

When chapter 20 opens, Andi is looking up from the San Joaquin Valley toward the mouth of a steep mountain canyon, the "Grapevine." The picture to the left shows the striking difference between the flat valley and the sudden rise of the Tehachapi Mountains. ("Tehachapi" is an Indian word meaning a "hard climb.")

The Tehachapi range divides the southern portion of California between the San Joaquin Valley to the northwest and the Mojave Desert in the southeast. The peaks range in height from 4,000—8,000 feet. The dramatic climb through the Grapevine canyon tops out at Tejon Pass. Tehachapi Pass, another mountain pass, connects the San Joaquin Valley to the Mojave Desert on the eastern edge of the mountains (where the famous Tehachapi railroad "loop" crosses).

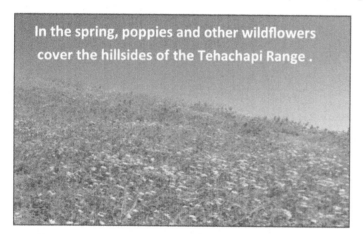

In the spring, poppies and other wildflowers cover the hillsides of the Tehachapi Range .

During the summer, the hills are dry and barren.

This is Castac Lake near the top of the mountains.

MAP WORK: The map to the right shows the southern portion of California. Based on the map on page 6 (in the book) and what you have learned here, label the indicated geographical features.

Los Angeles

WORD BOX
Tehachapi Mts.
Mojave Desert
Grapevine Canyon
San Joaquin Valley

1. _____

2. _____

3. _____

4. _____

HEARTBREAK TRAIL: FORT TEJON

Fort Tejon barracks

At the top of the Grapevine canyon, with an elevation of over 3,500 feet, lies a beautiful, tree-lined meadow, the site of Fort Tejon. Today the fort is a state historic site, but in 1854 it was a military outpost. Why establish a fort in the Tehachapi Mountains? A few years before, in 1849, the discovery of gold had drawn thousands of people into the area. With it came the inevitable clashes between the native people already living there, the miners, and the land-hungry settlers. The government set up a reservation at the southern end of the valley, along with a small army camp, but it lacked water, forage for the horses, and timber for construction. It was an altogether unsuitable spot (for both Indians and the army). The army moved seventeen miles into the mountains to a lovely site that contained everything needed to maintain a large military outpost. Civilians soon followed.

The soldiers (called Dragoons) patrolled a wide region: most of central and southern California, and sometimes clear to Utah. Their most-important duties included protecting the settlers, controlling the local Indians, and stopping raids from desert Indian bands. In 1859, the army took charge of a camel experiment and housed the beasts at Ft. Tejon. However, that did not last long. The animals were eventually sold or left to wander.

For ten years, Fort Tejon was a source of employment, protection, and social life for the local residents. When the Civil War broke out in 1861, the Dragoons were sent to guard Los Angeles and later transferred back East to fight. Only the local volunteer cavalry remained. The U.S. Army closed the fort in 1864, much to the disappointment of the locals. Edward Beale, a rancher, bought up most of the land in the area—including the fort grounds—in 1866. Today, the Tejon Ranch is one of the largest private land holdings in California.

FORT TEJON RIDDLES: WHO AM I?

Based on *Heartbreak Trail* and what is presented here, can you solve the following riddles?

1. I am a large building used to house the soldiers at Fort Tejon. _____

2. I am the route someone takes through the Tehachapi Mountains to arrive at Fort Tejon.

   _____   _____

3. We were the suffering participants of a failed experiment to improve transportation through the desert regions of the west. We died miserably. _____

4. Our duties were to protect the settlers and fend of Indian raids. _____

5. We never tired of participating in the fort's social activities. _____

71

Heartbreak Trail: Chapters 21–25

Show how well you understand the story by answering the following questions:

CHAPTERS 21-23

1. Label the following on the map on page 43 of the study guide:

   Santa Monica Mountains • Cahuenga Pass:) ([symbol for a pass] • Los Angeles

2. Andi is so angry at Toledo for trying to take liberties with her that she wants to run him down. What stops her from carrying out her plan?

   A. Levi is hurt and needs help. B. Toledo gallops away. C. Dusty swerves at the last second.

3. Andi's next "great" idea involves keeping Sultan away from Toledo so he can't chase after them. Is she successful with this plan? _____ Why or why not? _____

   _____

4. The loyal trail hands have had a bellyful of Toledo's behavior. Circle their reactions:

   "Aw, good riddance." • "Get out the six-shooters." • "Let's chase after him."

   "We need to get our beef back." • "He can't do any more harm. Let him go."

   "Let's hang him from the nearest tree." • "We should round up some men."

5. By now you should know who the permanent Circle C hands are and who are the temporary men. Circle the Circle C hands. Cross out the temporary trail hands. Wyatt • Toledo • Huey • Diego • Flint • Kirby • Cook • Tripp • Seth • Joselito • Bryce

6. Once the cattle are off Mitch's and Andi's hands, the story feels resolved. Sometimes an author throws in one last "twist" to surprise the reader. What is the twist in this story?

   _____

CHAPTERS 24-25

7. Where do Toledo, Huey, and the other two men take Andi and Levi? _____

8. How do Andi and Levi escape from their captivity?

   A. They kick and yell until somebody hears them.

   B. They cut their bonds with a knife from Levi's pocket.

   C. They crawl under the stall railings to freedom.

9. The first time Andi was asked what she wanted to do for her upcoming *quinceañera* she begged to go on the cattle drive. What does she hope to do now, if her mother gives her another chance to choose? _____

10. How do the Carters travel home?   A. horseback   B. railroad cars   C. stagecoach

HEARTBREAK TRAIL: HOW'S YOUR SPANISH? PART 4

Ten more Spanish words and phrases popped up back in chapters 17-20. Can you pronounce these words and match them without looking back?

1. _____ (p. 112) pronto (*práwn-toe*)

2. _____ (p. 113) bueno (*bwáy-no*)

3. _____ (p. 120) muy enojado (*moó-ie en-o-háh-doe*)

4. _____ (p. 122) Hasta mañana. (*áh-stuh mahn-yáh-na*)

5. _____ (p. 128) No se preocupe. (*no say pray-oh-coó-pay*)

6. _____ (p. 128) De nada. (*day náh-duh*)

7. _____ (p. 128) Lo siento. (*low see-én-toe*)

8. _____ (p. 129) ¡Ay no! (*I no*)

9. _____ (p. 129) tio (*teé-oh*)

10. _____ (p. 129) gracias (*gráh-see-ahs*)

A. See you tomorrow.

B. thank you

C. Don't worry.

D. I'm sorry.

E. very angry

F. uncle

G. Oh no!

H. you're welcome (it's nothing)

I. soon

J. good

ELEMENTS OF A FICTION STORY

Earlier in this study guide we looked at CHARACTERS and SETTING. Now let's touch on the overall story PROBLEM and the PLOT EVENTS up to this point.

1. Story Problem: The main character usually faces a number of conflicts as the story progresses. However, there is also one overshadowing problem that drives the hero/heroine and in the end causes some kind of character growth or change. What do you think is the main story problem Andi faces in *Heartbreak Trail*?

_____

_____

2. Plot Events: The other conflicts—great and small—make up the plot events. These are the situations the character faces as she strives toward the goal of coming to grips with the main story problem. Plot events form a pattern of "ups & downs" (good & bad) and give the story "pacing." Decide if the following plot events are an <u>up</u> or a <u>down</u> for Andi.

A. _____Andi learns that Levi gets to go on the trail drive. B. _____Andi receives permission to go along. C. _____ Andi has to ride Dusty instead of Taffy. D. _____Andi goes out to see the night herd. E. _____Toledo gives Andi a ride back to camp. F. _____Chad and Mitch scold Andi for going out to the herd alone. G. _____ Andi gets no sleep. H. _____ Andi takes a cool dunking in the pond. I. _____Everybody sits around the campfire telling stories. J. _____Andi almost drowns in the river. K. _____Cook fixes doughnuts. L. _____Chad is shot. M. _____Chad is taken to town and is okay.

Los Angeles stockyards

With a population of nearly four million, the City of Los Angeles (official name) is the second-largest city in the United States (after New York City). But what was this huge metropolis like when the Carters brought their 1,000 head of cattle to the city's stockyards?

The "City of Angels" began with forty-four persons (twenty-two adults and twenty-two children) as a Spanish settlement in 1781 along the banks of a river a Catholic priest had earlier named *Nuestra Señora de los Angeles de la Porciúncula* (Our Lady of the Angels of the Little Portion) in honor of a celebration and a chapel back home in Europe. The settlement was named after the river. It had a longer name at first: *El Pueblo de Nuestra Señora la Reina de los Angeles de Porciúncula* (The Town of Our Lady the Queen of Angels of the Little Portion). On page 151 in the book, young Rico uses the

Los Angeles in 1869

official "shortened" name, *El Pueblo de la Reina de Los Angeles*.

Mexico won its independence from Spain in 1821 and controlled the little town until the U.S. won all of the southwest from Mexico in 1847. At that time, the population of the little village was only 2,500 and nearly one-hundred percent *Californios* (Hispanic). Over the years, white Americans added to the population. By the time *Heartbreak Trail* takes place, Los Angeles had grown to a city of over 11,000 people.

"The Angels" is the English translation for *Los Angeles*. All over California and the Southwest, the names of cities reflect the highly religious Spanish explorers of the 18th and 19th centuries. Below are a number of Spanish-named cities in California and the Southwest. Can you figure out what the cities' names would be if the English names were used? You may be surprised at how many of them speak of Christ and His salvation. God was clearly on these Spanish explorers' minds as they established colonies and missions in the New World.

Blood of Christ	Mountain of the King	Riverview	Sacrament	St. John the Baptist
The Cats	Holy Faith	Saint Matthew	The Crosses	Butterfly	Holy Cross	The Tar

1. Mariposa _____

2. La Brea _____

3. Los Gatos _____

4. Sacramento _____

5. Santa Cruz _____

6. San Juan Bautista

_____

7. Rio Vista _____

8. Santa Fe _____

9. Las Cruces _____

10. Monterey _____

11. San Mateo _____

12. Sangre de Cristo (mountains)

_____

I didn't think I would care that Levi watched the train go up and around the famous Tehachapi Loop while I slept. That's all he talked about from Bakersfield to Fresno, and I got mighty tired of it. But when Mitch agreed and called it one of the wonders of the railroad world, I began to think I missed something special.

HEARTBREAK TRAIL: THE TEHACHAPI LOOP

What is this famous "wonder of the railroad world" Levi couldn't stop talking about all the way back to the ranch? It is a 3/4 mile-long spiral of railroad track halfway up the grade to the Tehachapi Pass. It connects the city of Mojave in the Mojave Desert with Bakersfield in the San Joaquin Valley. It is one of the busiest single tracks in the entire world.

One of the engineering feats of its day, the Southern Pacific Railroad built the Loop to ease the steep grade going over the Tehachapi Mountains. Three thousand Chinese workers cut through solid granite with picks, shovels, horse-drawn carts, and blasting powder. The railroad line, of which the Loop is a part, had eighteen tunnels, ten bridges, and a number of water towers to refill the locomotives as they steamed over the Tehachapi Mountains.

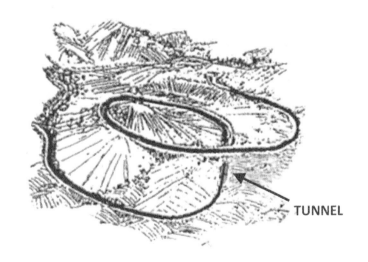

TUNNEL

Work began in 1874 and took two years to complete. This track line was the final piece in the railroad linking San Francisco to Los Angeles. When Andi and her family rode over the Loop, it had been in operation for eight years. This same track line has remained virtually unchanged since it was first constructed. It is indeed an amazing display of engineering genius.

WEB FUN:

Copy this link to watch a YouTube video showing a modern train tackling the Loop:

www.youtube.com/watch?v=-UWm2PAJkQU

Seven engines pull 111 cars. Start at 1:00 and watch at least until 5:30. The train goes over itself in the tunnel and comes close to the screen as it makes its way to Mojave.

Daily Schedule for Book 3: The Last Ride

*indicates an optional activity found in the *Circle C Milestones* lapbook.
(Lapbook activities can be skipped or purchased from **CircleCAdventures.com**)

	Day 1	Day 2	Day 3	Day 4
The Last Ride	Chapters 1-2	Chapters 3	Chapters 4-5	— — — — —
Literature Guide	Page 77	Page 79 #1-6	Page 79 #7-11	*Lapbook activity for chapters 1-5*
	Day 5	**Day 6**	**Day 7**	**Day 8**
The Last Ride	— — — — —	— — — — —	Chapters 6-7	Chapters 8-9
Literature Guide	Pages 80-82	Pages 83-85	Page 86 #1-5	Page 86 #6-8 Page 87
	Day 9	**Day 10**	**Day 11**	**Day 12**
The Last Ride	— — — — —	— — — — —	— — — — —	Chapters 10-11
Literature Guide	Pages 88-90	*Lapbook activity 1 for chapters 6-9*	*Lapbook activity 2 for chapters 6-9*	Page 91 #1-8
	Day 13	**Day 14**	**Day 15**	**Day 16**
The Last Ride	Chapters 12-13	— — — — —	— — — — —	Chapter 14
Literature Guide	Page 91 #9-13 Page 92	*Lapbook activity for chapters 10-13*	Pages 93-95	Pages 96-97
	Day 17	**Day 18**	**Day 19**	**Day 20**
The Last Ride	Chapter 15	Chapters 16-17	— — — — —	— — — — —
Literature Guide	Page 98 #1-6	Page 98 #7-14	Pages 99-101	*Lapbook activity for chapters 14-17*
	Day 21	**Day 22**	**Day 23**	**Day 24**
The Last Ride	Chapters 18-19	Chapters 20-21	— — — — —	— — — — —
Literature Guide	Page 102 #1-7	Page 102 #8-15 Page 103	Pages 104-106	*Lapbook activity for chapters 18-21*
	Day 25	**Day 26**	**Day 27**	**Day 28**
The Last Ride	Chapters 22-24	Chapters 25-26	— — — — —	— — — — —
Literature Guide	Page 107 #1-8	Page 107 #9-17	Pages 108-111	*Lapbook activity for chapters 22-26*

Story Synopsis: The Last Ride opens just before Andi turns sixteen. At long last she can start helping Chad manage the ranch and have time to train Taffy's colt Shasta. A wrinkle appears when Chad hires Riley Prescott to work with the young stock, but Andi sets aside her annoyance when Cousin Daniel arrives from New York City. His parents have sent him to the Circle C in hopes that family out west can help turn the boy around. Welcoming Daniel turns Andi's world upside down. He hates everything about the ranch, comes and goes as he pleases, and exasperates Andi, who has agreed to teach him ranch skills. When Andi discovers a secret Daniel is harboring, he forces her to remain silent. Daniel's actions climax in a life-shattering accident that threatens to tear the Carter family apart. Is forgiveness even possible?

The character quality/theme for *The Last Ride* is "forgiveness." In your best handwriting, copy Colossians 3:13 from page 3 in the book. Color, cut out the poster, and memorize this verse during your study.

FORGIVENESS:

A DELIBERATE DECISION TO LET GO OF RESENTMENT TOWARD AN OFFENDER

The Last Ride: Chapters 1–5

CHAPTERS 1-3

1. Receiving a letter in the 1800s was a big event. What is the origin of this particular letter?
_____ Who is the letter from? _____

2. The letter from New York introduces the reader to a line-up of characters in the story. Match the characters with their descriptions.

_____ Lydia   A. I am a new baby boy, born at Thanksgiving time last year.

_____ Benjamin   B. I am one of Taffy's twins foals.

_____ Rebecca   C. I am Andi and Melinda's oldest sister. I live in San Francisco.

_____ Justin   D. I live with my family in New York. Rebecca is my older sister.

_____ Daniel   E. I am happily married and live in town with my wife and son.

_____ Lucy   F. I have never married but involve myself in my family's lives.

_____ Samuel   G. My husband and I are concerned about our son's welfare.

_____ Katherine   H. I am very happy to have married into the Carter family.

_____ Shasta   I. I am a cousin the Carter family has hardly ever see.

3. Sid McCoy greets Andi with some unwelcome news. What is it? _____
_____

4. What is the name of the new wrangler Chad has hired? _____

5. According to Melinda, how many years has it been since Aunt Lydia, Uncle Benjamin, and Daniel visited the ranch? _____ What was the reason for that visit?
_____

6. Name three things Daniel did as a young boy to harass his girl cousins:
_____ _____ _____

CHAPTERS 4-5

7. Circle the brother whom Daniel resembles: Justin   •   Chad   •   Mitch

8. Circle the two things Aunt Rebecca always seems to badger Andi about.

not wearing long skirts   •   not protecting her skin   •   always running

her nickname, Andi   •   not wearing a corset   •   for being disrespectful

9. What does Andi hope she and Daniel have in common? _____

10. Andi's father died ten years ago. How was he killed? _____

11. What is another name for a "cotillion"? _____

THE LAST RIDE: PANDORA'S BOX-WHY IS THERE EVIL IN THE WORLD?

On pages 23 and 24, Andi says, "I can't help it. I reckon I'm just like that Pandora character in the Greek mythology book Mr. Foster assigned. I've got too much curiosity for my own good."

What did Andi mean by her statement? Who is Pandora? And what does she have to do with curiosity?

Like so many ancient cultures that abandoned the truth of God's Word, the Greeks (and Romans) made up their own stories (myths) to explain what they saw in the world around them. They had a story for everything, and some are quite interesting and fun to read. Did you ever wonder how the constellation of Orion got its name? The Greeks had a story to explain how the mighty hunter ended up in the sky. Even the planets are named after various gods and goddesses of Greek and Roman myths.

The story of Pandora is their explanation for how evil (or sin) entered the world.

The story of Pandora dates back to about 700 or 800 BC (before Christ). After mankind received the stolen gift of fire from Prometheus (a story for another time), an angry Zeus (the chief god) gave them a punishing gift to compensate for this great gift of fire they now had. From clay was molded the first woman, a "beautiful evil," whose descendants would torment the human race. The other gods and goddesses on Mount Olympus gave her gifts: Aphrodite gave her beauty, Apollo bestowed on her the gift of music, Athena presented silver gowns and necklaces. Hera gave the woman a curious nature. Hermes gave her the name Pandora, meaning "all-gifted."

Pandora eventually married, and Zeus gifted her with a locked box as a wedding present (the Greek word should really be translated "jar"). He told her she should *never* open that box, but Pandora's curiosity overruled her good sense. Every time she walked by the beautiful box, she wondered what was inside. Clothes? Jewelry? She begged her husband for the key, but he always said no. She so longed to see what was inside that one day when her husband was sleeping, she stole the key and sneaked a peek.

Instantly, out sprang all kinds of evil to infect the world: sickness, famine, hate, envy, and every wickedness one could imagine. And death. Pandora cried out and slammed the lid shut, but it was too late. Death and evil had entered the world. The "golden age" was over. But to her surprise, there was one good thing that trailed out of the box last: hope.

Was there ever really hope? The story never says. Unlike the Bible, which is full of hope, there is no happy ending for mankind in the story of Pandora's Box.

THE LAST RIDE: GOD'S WORD, THE SOURCE OF ALL TRUTH

It's astonishing how people will make up their own version of the truth rather than accept God's instructions laid out in the Bible. Do they really think they can avoid facing the Creator one day if they simply refuse to believe He is the "I AM," the one, true God?

Read Genesis 3 (yes, the whole chapter) to learn the real reason sin entered the world. Not only does the Genesis account give the sad, hard facts, but Genesis 3:15 also gives mankind a hope the ancient Greeks did not have.

Although the Bible tells the true story, the two accounts do share similarities. This makes it likely that after the fall and the flood, ancient people groups took the creation account and the fall of man with them as they spread out over the earth (like they took the Flood account with them). But that knowledge was clearly twisted as the years went by, and much was forgotten.

Using the Scriptures given in parentheses and the story from the previous page, find the similarities between the two accounts and fill out the chart.

THE ACCOUNTS	GREEK MYTH	SCRIPTURE
Who was the first woman?		(Genesis 3:20)
How was she created?		(Genesis 2:22)
What command was given to each of them?		(Genesis 2:16-17)
Whom did each disobey?		(Genesis 3:13)
How did each disobey?		(Genesis 3:6)
What was the result of disobedience?		(Romans 5:12)
What hope was given for mankind?		(Colossians 1:27)

THE LAST RIDE: VOCABULARY & GRAMMAR

For each underlined word below, write the part of speech (noun, verb, or adjective) on the line. Then choose the best definition for how the word is used in the sentence.

1. Melinda <u>prattled on</u> about shopping for fashions in Paris. _____VERB_____

    A. bragged   B. complained   Ⓒ. chattered   D. gossiped

2. Andi loved her sister, but sometimes Melinda could be <u>maddening</u>. _____

    A. exasperating   B. pleasing   C. impatient   D. impolite

3. Charges had been brought over an <u>alleged</u> assault. _____

    A. confirmed   B. supposed   C. dangerous   D. intended

4. Andi laughed at her colt's <u>antics</u>. _____

    A. jumps   B. moves   C. beauty   D. tricks

5. Andi stared at Riley, <u>dumbstruck</u>. _____

    A. scared half to death   C. angry as all get-out

    B. speechless with surprise   D. full of sorrow

6. "You tore into the letter, which planted <u>uncharitable</u> thoughts in your mind." _____

    A. unkind   B. loving   C. generous   D. unapologetic

7. Daniel had caught her. Andi *had* meant to be a <u>tad</u> saucy. _____

    A. a passing   B. a lot more   C. a little bit   D. a touch put off

8. Andi <u>yearned</u> to sit up front in the surrey, chattering nonstop with Justin. _____

    A. preferred   B. greatly desired   C. begged   D. appealed

9. Daniel's loud <u>guffaw</u> caused Aunt Rebecca to turn around. _____

    A. laugh   B. complaint   C. roar   D. protest

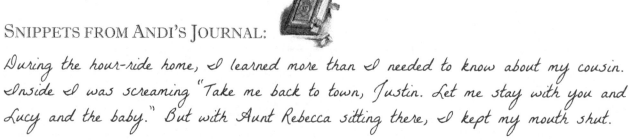

SNIPPETS FROM ANDI'S JOURNAL:

During the hour-ride home, I learned more than I needed to know about my cousin. Inside I was screaming "Take me back to town, Justin. Let me stay with you and Lucy and the baby." But with Aunt Rebecca sitting there, I kept my mouth shut.

FROM SEA TO SHINING SEA: THE TRANSCONTINENTAL RAILROAD

In an age when we can hop on a plane and fly 3,000 miles across the United States in less than a day, it's hard to imagine how long it took to travel from New York to California in the 1800s. Before 1869, it took weeks to cross the rivers, mountains, and vast plains by wagon or stagecoach. The trip was full of danger, hunger, and boredom. Thanks to the transcontinental railroad, however, Aunt Rebecca and Daniel made the trip from New York to California in six days rather than six weeks. They owed their thanks for this railroad to two companies' vision.

About ten years after California became a state in 1850, two railroad companies—the Central Pacific (based in California) and the Union Pacific on the other side of the country—dreamed of linking the United States from sea to sea. The two companies decided to "race" to see who could lay the most track, and they would meet in the middle. Governor Leland Stanford broke ground for the Central Pacific's eastbound tracks in January 1863 in Sacramento, the capital of California.

The Central Pacific got a two-year head start, and they needed it. Tunneling through the mighty Sierra Nevada range would take many months. It was easy to lay track in the flat Central Valley, but construction slowed down in the foothills and nearly came to a standstill in the mountains. Tunnels were constructed the hard way: workmen drilled holes with sledgehammers, stuffed blasting powder into the holes, and blew the boulders up—about a foot a day.

Many people died from avalanches and explosions. The Central Pacific hired thousands of Chinese laborers. They were untiring workers, and worked for between one and three dollars a day doing *very* dangerous work. The Chinese blasted fifteen tunnels for the Central Pacific.

The Union Pacific's westbound tracks began slower. They had to compete with the War Between the States for workers, rails, railroad engines, and other supplies. They basically ended up waiting until the war was over in 1865 to begin their race from Omaha, Nebraska, but the flat plains were an easier place to lay tracks.

The east coast already had a fine collection of train routes stretching all the way to Nebraska, so Omaha was the Union Pacific's starting point. Many of the workers were Irish immigrants, and most of the work consisted of laying track and driving the spikes. Other men strung telegraph lines. Cooks prepared meals, and clerks kept the accounts. Engineers, carpenters, blacksmiths, and surveyors were busy day and night. All work was done by hand: shovels, picks, axes, black powder, and wheelbarrows, ropes, mules, and horses.

On May 10, 1869, in Promontory, Utah, Leland Stanford drove the "golden spike" that connected the Union Pacific and Central Pacific RR tracks. A train traveling from the west met the train traveling from the east, and the transcontinental railroad was born. After completing their four-to-six years' work on the railroad, the laborers returned to their previous lives. Many Chinese worked for other railroads, some took their money and returned to China, and others sent for their families and settled in California.

83

THE LAST RIDE: THE GREAT RAILROAD RACE-THE ROUTE

On the map below, the route of the transcontinental railroad is laid out.

Using an atlas or Internet resource:

1. Label the states the new transcontinental railroad race passed through. (Use postal abbreviations. See example for California.)

2. Label Sacramento (in California).

3. Label New York City (in New York).

4. Label Omaha (in Nebraska).

5. Label Promontory (in Utah).

6. Use a BROWN colored pencil to shade the location of the Sierra Nevada range.

7. Use a RED pencil to color the Central Pacific Railroad's route.

8. Use a BLUE pencil to color the Union Pacific Railroad's route.

9. Using blue and red pencils, label the Map Key with the Central Pacific route and the Union Pacific's route.

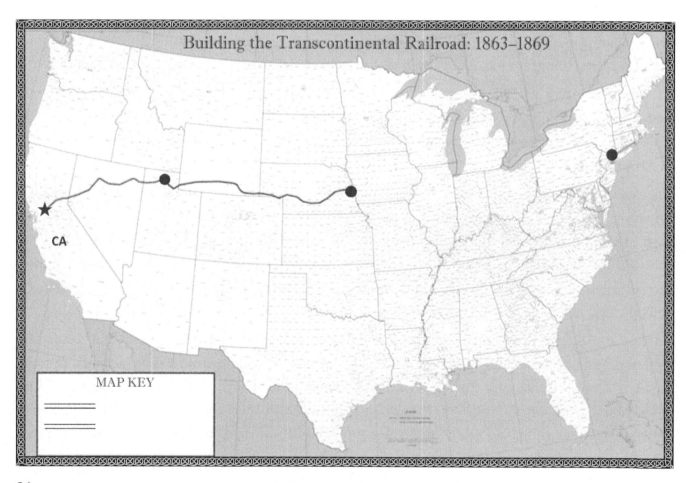

Building the Transcontinental Railroad: 1863–1869

CA

MAP KEY

THE LAST RIDE: THE GREAT RAILROAD RACE-THE MATH

The race to lay track was a serious one for the Union and Central Pacific railroads. The U.S. government gave the companies land and money based on how much track they laid over the land. Each railroad company rushed to lay track and "claim" their miles.

1. The **Union Pacific** laid 1,087 miles of track. The **Central Pacific** laid 690 miles of track. Who "won" the great railroad race? _____

   By how many miles did they win? _____

2. The new transcontinental railroad stretched from Omaha, Nebraska, to Sacramento, California. Using the miles from #1 above, how many **total miles** did the new route stretch? _____ miles

3. The original plan stated that fifty miles of track must be laid the first year. If they had continued with this "fifty miles of track per year" plan, about how many years would it have taken the Union and Pacific railroads to build the transcontinental railroad? _____ years. (Use the total miles of track from problem #2 and divide by fifty.)

4. It reality, how long did it take to finish the unbroken line of track from east to west? _____ years. (Look back on the information page to find out when the Central Pacific broke ground and when the final golden spike was driven to complete the line. Subtract the two dates to find the number of years.)

5. On an "easy day," the railroad companies could lay a mile or more of track a day. The Central Pacific railroad went a little crazy toward the end of the race. They laid ten miles of track in *one day!* If they could have kept this up, how many miles of tracks could they have laid in seven days?

   _____ miles of track

The Last Ride: Chapters 6–9

CHAPTERS 6–7

1. Match the Spanish words with their English meanings:

_____ *Gracias*   A. Is there a problem?

_____ *De nada*   B. Welcome.

_____ *señor*   C. I don't know.

_____ *Bienvenido*   D. sir / mister

_____ *Hay un problema?* E. You're welcome.

_____ *No sé.*   F. Thank you.

> **Spanish Lesson**
>
> "Jesus loves me. The Bible says so" goes like this in Spanish:
>
> Cristo me ama. (*Creés-toe may ah-ma*)
>
> La Biblia dice así.
>
> (*Lah Beé-blee-ah deé-say ah-seé*)

2. "Continental manners" is a term used when referring to how people greet one another on the European continent (across the Atlantic Ocean). Which aspect of these manners does Andi feel silly for overreacting to earlier? (Circle your answer.)

    A. bowing and curtsying   B. hugs and cheek-kissing   C. bowing and hand-kissing

3. What is one of Andi's worst "sins"? _____

4. Circle the two things Daniel believes one must have to find a good place in high society.

    A. money and charm   B. beauty and a good name   C. money and intelligence

5. When Aunt Rebecca collapses and Mother asks Andi to send somebody for the doctor, what recent invention does Andi wish her family had access to? _____

CHAPTERS 8–9

6. Nitroglycerin is an unstable explosive. However, in tiny doses, even today it works miracles for people with a heart condition. Circle the effects a nitroglycerin tablet has:

    lowers blood pressure • speeds up a sluggish heart • dilates blood vessels

    keeps the heart from working too hard • prevents dizziness • stops the heart

7. Why does Andi control her tongue and quietly submit to Aunt Rebecca's demands at breakfast the next morning? _____

8. Andi quotes part of a Bible verse to Daniel about charm being deceptive.

Look up Proverbs 31:30 and copy the verse in the box below.

THE LAST RIDE: VOCABULARY–LOTS OF SYNONYMS

For each underlined word below, circle **all** of the synonyms for that word. Cross out any words that are *not* synonyms. (See example.)

1. "I apologize for my <u>boorish</u> behavior those many years ago," Daniel said.

(rude) (ill-mannered) (crude) (mean) ~~polite~~ (discourteous) ~~boring~~

2. "You must be exhausted after that <u>grueling</u> train ride," Mother told Aunt Rebecca.

relaxing strenuous tiring easy difficult scenic refreshing

3. Andi wanted to run to the barn to get away from Aunt Rebecca's constant <u>harping</u>.

whispering pestering tormenting bothering giggling coughing badgering

4. Her brothers and a few ranch hands <u>converged on</u> Andi from the corrals and buildings.

joined met ran away from gathered around irritated

5. "It <u>dilates</u> the blood vessels and lowers pressure so the heart doesn't have to work hard."

enlarges contracts narrows opens widens expands

6. "The trouble is," Andi wrote, "everything I do seems to <u>agitate</u> Aunt Rebecca."

bother calm excite stir up irritate soothe annoy

7. Rebecca lowered her teacup and <u>scrutinized</u> Andi's attire.

glanced at inspected examined waved away looked closely at

8. Mother <u>pursed</u> her lips but did not contradict her sister-in-law.

compressed opened puckered squeezed relaxed tightened

9. "Doctor Weaver was <u>adamant</u> yesterday. We must keep Aunt Rebecca quiet."

confused firm worried insistent unyielding unbendable

10. "I don't suppose your <u>provincial</u> village has electricity yet," Daniel scoffed.

simple rural advanced backward up-to-date modern

GEOGRAPHY: 1882 RAILROAD ROUTES By 1884, the transcontinental railroad had expanded to many routes, connecting a good portion of the populated western states with the Atlantic states back east. On the map, circle the stops the Carters made on their trip out West. (See stops in the white box below). At each stop, they have to make a decision to either stay on the train or board a new route in a new direction. Sometimes they buy something. Write what they do at each stop. Use compass directions.

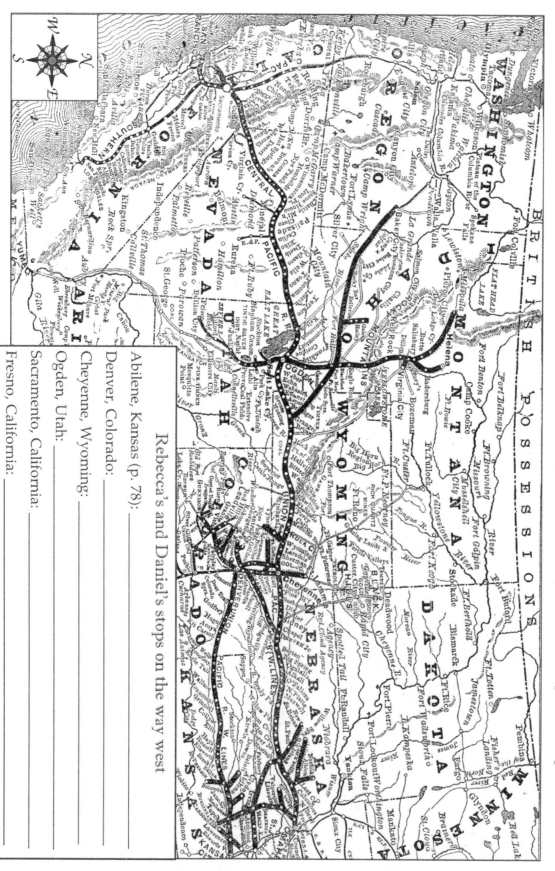

Rebecca's and Daniel's stops on the way west

Abilene, Kansas (p. 78): _____

Denver, Colorado: _____

Cheyenne, Wyoming: _____

Ogden, Utah: _____

Sacramento, California: _____

Fresno, California: _____

88

THE LAST RIDE: NEW YORK CITY

Uncle Benjamin, Aunt Lydia, and their son, Daniel, live in the largest city in the United States: New York. Originally called "New Amsterdam," it began as a Dutch trading post in 1624 on the island of Manhattan. The English took control of the post in 1664 and renamed it "New York." Later, from 1785 until 1790, New York served as the capital of the United States.

New Amsterdam trading post - 1660

New York City is made up of five boroughs: **Brooklyn, Queens, Manhattan, The Bronx,** and **Staten Island**. Until they were combined in 1898, these five boroughs were five separate, distinct cities. The East River Bridge (Brooklyn Bridge) was completed in 1883 and connected the city of Brooklyn to that of Manhattan (where Daniel and his family live). Manhattan is the busy, skyscraper section of New York City and also home to Central Park.

GEOGRAPHY

Use an atlas or the Internet to familiarize yourself with the geography of New York state and New York City. On the map of the United States, find and label your state (if you live in the Continental U.S.). Find New York state and color it green. List the states that border New York:

1. _____

2. _____

3. _____

4. _____

5. _____

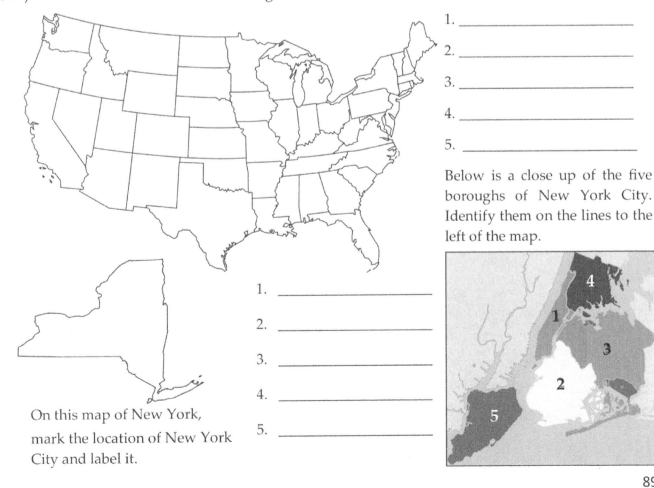

Below is a close up of the five boroughs of New York City. Identify them on the lines to the left of the map.

1. _____

2. _____

3. _____

4. _____

5. _____

On this map of New York, mark the location of New York City and label it.

THE LAST RIDE: THE BROOKLYN BRIDGE

Daniel bragged to Andi about watching the East River Bridge go up. Construction began in 1869 and was completed in 1883—fourteen years later. It is one of the oldest bridges in the United States and full of passageways and compartments. The bridge connects the city of Brooklyn with Manhattan. The day it opened, President Chester Arthur was on hand for the ceremonies, along with 150,000+ people who crossed the bridge. The bridge was a huge accomplishment for the American people and the longest suspension bridge in the world at that time.

The bridge carried horse-drawn traffic and rails (trains), as well as a separate, elevated walkway for pedestrians and bicycles. Six days after the bridge opened, rumors went around that it was going to collapse. People panicked, and twelve were killed in the stampede to get off the bridge. A year later, P.T. Barnum of circus fame squashed doubts about the bridge's safety by leading his most famous elephant, Jumbo, along with twenty-one other elephants across the bridge.

Because of its excellent design, the Brooklyn Bridge (officially so named in 1915) is still standing, when other bridges built at that time have vanished into history.

WEB FUN: Ride the train with Thomas Edison over the Brooklyn Bridge from Brooklyn to New York City in this two-minute, 1899 video (copy the link carefully):
https://upload.wikimedia.org/wikipedia/commons/2/2d/New_Brooklyn_to_New_York_via_Brooklyn_Bridge%2C_no._2%2C_by_Thomas_A._Edison%2C_Inc.ogv

New York City (Manhattan) in 1873

The East River (Brooklyn) Bridge

The Last Ride: Chapters 10–13

CHAPTERS 10–11

1. What does Daniel do that throws Andi into a panic? _____

_____

2. At first, Andi decides to hang onto her seat and trust God to hold the buggy together. What
   changes her mind and prods her into taking action to stop the ride?

_____

3. True or False (circle your answer): Andi wins the wrestling match for control of the buggy.

4. Circle the results of Andi and Daniel's wild ride: • Andi nearly loses her breakfast •

   Daniel is apologetic • Andi is thrown from the rig • the buggy's axle cracks •

   they have to walk to town • Andi receives cuts • the buggy crashes into a peach tree

5. Before Andi can say a word, Justin asks, "What's the trouble?" Two clues give away the fact
   that he knows something is troubling his sister. What are they?

_____

_____

6. Who hauls the buggy out of Mallards' orchard and back to town? _____

7. What do Johnny Wilson and Daniel have in common? _____

_____

8. Chad and Justin scold Andi and Daniel for the buggy mishap. Then Chad assigns Daniel to
   work with Diego. What does he tell Andi to do? _____

CHAPTERS 12–13

9. Riley recognizes Daniel from when the two of them were little boys. What does Riley
   remember doing to Daniel? _____

10. Why is Andi angry when she catches Daniel in Taffy's stall? _____

_____

11. What does Andi try to teach Daniel to lasso? _____

12. True or False: Daniel abandons his lassoing lesson and goes to town without permission.

13. Who offers to accompany Aunt Rebecca home to San Francisco?

   A. Daniel   B. Justin   C. Melinda   D. Mother

THE LAST RIDE: VOCABULARY-MATCHING

Match the underlined word in each phrase with the correct meaning. Page numbers where the word is first used are given so you can find the meaning using the context of the sentence. The first one has been done for you.

SECTION A:

1. __D__ the frenzy of a thrill seeker (p. 65)

2. _____ exhilarating (p. 66)

3. _____ to cower in a corner (p. 66)

4. _____ to snub someone (p. 68)

5. _____ to infuriate someone (p. 74)

6. _____ to reminisce (p. 77)

7. _____ to look contrite (p. 79)

8. _____ his high-handed superiority (p. 83)

9. _____ to muff the toss (p. 86)

10. _____ to be adept (p. 86)

11. _____ an invalid (p. 88)

A. thrilling; exciting

B. to brush off; ignore

C. overconfidence; self-importance

D. ~~passion and emotion~~

E. to remember; to ponder

F. to make angry

G. to shrink away; to cringe

H. a sick person

I. to be skillful; expert

J. sorry; regretful

DIGGING DEEPER

The Carter family made a commitment to help turn Daniel around. It was common practice in the 19th century to send rebellious children to relatives for a fresh start. Sometimes it worked. Sometimes it didn't. How far do you think families should go to help one another? Is there a point where it is okay to say "enough is enough"? Give at least one reason for your answer.

_____

_____

_____

Andi has no say in the decision to bring Daniel to the ranch. Do you agree that the adults only should decide if a relative comes to live with you? Or should all members of the family have a say in such an important decision? Give a reason for your answer:

_____

_____

_____

THE LAST RIDE: CHARACTER CLUES

Can you identify the characters from *The Last Ride* by the following clues?

1. I cannot understand why my family does not display proper manners and behavior. It's embarrassing to be seen in public with my youngest niece. When will she grow up? _____

2. I've had to grow up mighty fast the past eight years. Roaming around the country from fort to fort, I've seen more than my fair share of trouble and drama. I hope to stay on the Circle C a long time.

   _____

3. I'm not excited *at all* to be staying on the Circle C. _____

4. I run the ranch for my bosses, Chad and Mitch. _____

5. I know how to soothe our aunt when she gets on her high horse about proper behavior:

   _____

6. I've met my match as far as getting someone to pull their weight around the ranch. I'm ready to pack a certain young man up and send him home. _____

7. I want nothing more than to help manage the Circle C ranch. I'm not sure I can do it, though. I can't even manage one cousin. _____

8. I've recently been born into the adventurous Carter family. _____

CHARACTER SKETCH

Choose one of the characters from the activity above and write a brief character sketch about them. A character sketch includes physical and personality traits (quiet, outgoing, loving, shy, etc.) as well as character traits (hardworking, boastful, honest, etc.).

Character: _____

_____

_____

_____

_____

_____

_____

_____

THE LAST RIDE: WORLD'S FAIRS

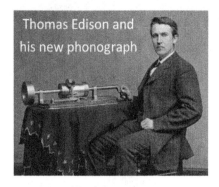
Thomas Edison and his new phonograph

At the end of chapter 9, Daniel asks Andi why her family did not travel to the recent International Exposition in Paris so she could see "all things electric." If Andi had gone to Paris, she would have seen the telephone, Thomas Edison's new phonograph, electric streetlights, and the newly finished head of the Statue of Liberty on display.

Lady Liberty's head at the 1878 Paris world's fair.

World's fairs—or International Expositions as they are sometimes called—have been around since the early 1800s. The first one was held in 1844 in Paris, France. The rest of Europe soon began hosting the fairs. England put on "The Great Exhibition" in 1851. During the 19th century (and even into the 20th century), world's fairs were famous for displaying technological inventions (like the telephone, electric lights, and even solar power) and bringing science and technology from around the world together in one location.

The United States has hosted a number of world's fairs: New York (1853 & 1939), Philadelphia (1876), Chicago (1893 & 1933), New Orleans (1884 & 1984), St. Louis (1904), San Francisco (1915 & 1939), and Seattle (1909 & 1962) to name a few.

After 1939, expositions began to depart from their original focus on technology. Inventions and scientific advancements were not the primary displays. Instead, many expositions showcased cultural themes like "Building the World of Tomorrow" and "Peace Through Understanding."

When a city hosts a world's fair, it can have long-lasting effects on the community. For example, the 1962 world's fair (Century 21 Exposition) was held in Seattle, Washington. The race for the moon was in full swing, and the Expo's motto was "Living in the Space Age." A monorail and "Space Needle" were specially constructed for the Expo. To this day, Seattle is known for its space needle left over from the world's fair.

New Orleans hosted the last world's fair in the United States in 1984. Since then, world's fairs continue to exhibit around the world but not in the U.S. Attending a world's fair is a memorable experience. Mrs. Marlow, the author of the Circle C Milestones, attended the Seattle World's Fair in 1962, and she has never forgotten it. Going to the top of the space needle and riding the monorail are still exciting experiences for visitors.

THE LAST RIDE: WHERE IN THE WORLD?

World's fairs are held all over the world. Below is a map of the world. Using the Internet or an atlas, locate and color the COUNTRIES that have hosted a world's fair. See list below the map.

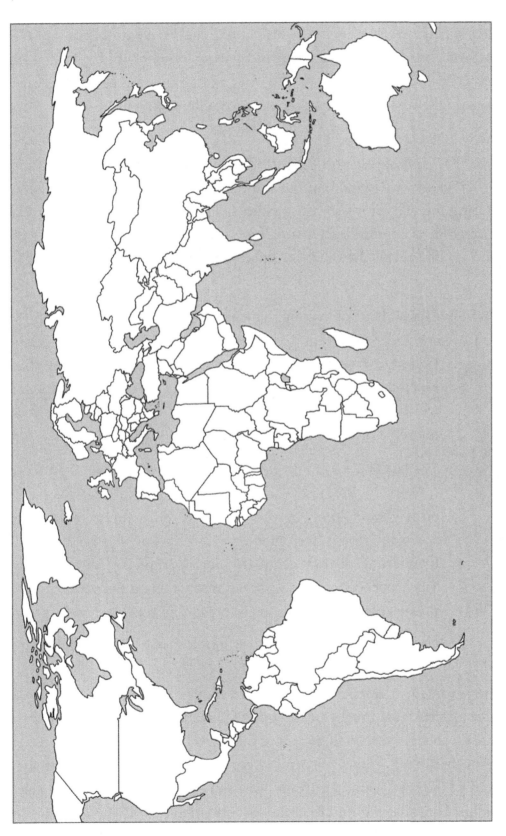

Paris, France (1855): LAVENDAR

Sydney, Australia (1879): GRAY

Rio de Janeiro, Brazil (1922): TAN

Hannover, Germany (2000): PINK

New York, U.S. (1853): RED

Vienna, Austria (1873): BLUE

Milan, Italy (1906): GREEN

Osaka, Japan (1970): ORANGE

London, England (1851): BLACK

Porto, Portugal (1865): BROWN

Barcelona, Spain (1888): PURPLE

Montreal, Canada (1967): YELLOW

THE LAST RIDE: FRANK AND JESSE JAMES

Jesse James

Andi mentions the outlaws Frank and Jesse James at the end of chapter ten and compares her cousin Daniel and her former classmate, Johnny Wilson, to them. By the time 1884 rolled around, Jesse James had been dead two years, and Frank James had given himself up. They never robbed or killed in California, but Andi knows all about them, as probably did everyone else in the country. They were among the most notorious outlaws of the American West and the first to rob a bank in broad daylight (1866).

Who were these brothers? Frank James was the elder, born in 1843. Jesse came along four years later in 1847. Brought up on a Missouri farm, the boys shared their family's sympathy for the Southern "cause" when the War Between the States broke out in 1861 (Jesse was only 14 at the time). During the war, Frank joined a band called "Quantrill's Raiders," a group thought to have massacred two hundred men and boys in Lawrence, Kansas, a center of abolitionists (people who wanted to free the slaves). Apparently, William Quantrill and the James boy didn't like this idea of freeing the slaves.

After the war, the James boys formed their own gang, which lasted about ten years (from 1866 to 1876). Jesse James didn't become well-known until 1869, when he and Frank robbed a bank in

Frank & Jesse James

Gallatin, Missouri. They didn't get much money, but Jesse shot and killed the cashier. Not good! This robbery and killing marked Jesse for the first time as an "outlaw," and the governor of Missouri offered a reward for his capture.

The James gang might have lasted longer, but an attempted bank robbery in Minnesota went bad, and several members of their outlaw band were captured or killed. They continued their crime wave, recruiting fresh members, but the law was hot on their trail by this time. So they had to do a lot of hiding and sneaking around. They robbed trains, as well, but rarely robbed the passengers. They preferred to get right to the Express safe in the baggage car.

Unfortunately, Jesse James's outlaw days were numbered. On April 3, 1882, he was killed by Robert Ford, a member of his own gang. Apparently, Robert wanted to cash in on the reward money being offered. It came as a complete surprise to Jesse. He had just finished eating breakfast and was getting ready to travel to Platte City for a planned robbery. Jesse walked across the living room to lay his revolvers on a sofa. He turned around to brush off a dusty picture. Robert Ford drew his pistol and shot the unarmed Jesse in the back of the head. Upon his death, Jesse James—who was already a celebrity in life—became a legendary figure throughout the Midwest and the West.

FRANK AND JESSE JAMES—CONTINUED

A few months after his brother was killed, Frank James gave himself up to the law. He was tried for murder in Missouri and, amazingly, was found not guilty. He was tried for robbery in Alabama. The verdict: not guilty. Once again, he was tried for armed robbery in Missouri and again released. A free man at last, Frank retired to a quiet life on his family's old farm, where he lived until his death in 1915, dying in the room in which he was born.

Frank James, 1898

Frank & Jesse James Crossword Puzzle

ACROSS:

2. the man who killed Jesse James
5. one who supports freedom for slaves
6. the younger James brother, killed in 1882
9. the leader of a raider gang during the War Between the States
10. the older James brother, died in 1915
11. a state where Frank James was found not guilty
12. the bank robbery that made Jesse famous occurred here

DOWN:

1. the name of a kind of safe kept in the baggage car on a train
3. the state where the James gang never committed a crime
4. the James brothers were born in this state
7. the state where a robbery went bad
8. another word for a criminal

Word Bank
outlaw
Express
Gallatin
California
Alabama
Quantrill
Jesse
Frank
Missouri
Minnesota
Ford
abolitionist

Created with The Teachers Corner.net Crossword Maker

The Last Ride: Chapters 14–17

CHAPTERS 14–15

1. What bad news do Andi and Justin learn when they pick up Daniel from the train depot?

   A. He is battered and disheveled.   B. He's not there.   C. He has brought home a friend.

2. Circle the family members who would like to leave Daniel in the city. Draw a box around those who feel he needs to be brought back. Cross out the family members who appear to have no opinion about the matter:

   Mother • Justin • Chad • Mitch • Melinda • Andi • Lucy

3. List four terrible things that could have happened to Daniel in San Francisco (pp. 92–93):

   _____   _____

   _____   _____

4. What are the two parts to Daniel's punishment? A) _____

   B) _____

5. Why does Andi praise God with *Your works are marvelous indeed* the next Sunday?

   _____

6. What does Cory accuse Daniel of doing? _____

CHAPTERS 16–17

7. What is the secret Andi can't tell anybody? _____

8. What does Daniel threaten to do if Andi tells? _____

9. Name some of the items Andi discovers in Daniel's "loot." _____

   _____

10. Each morning Andi is filled with resolve to tell Chad about Daniel. What happens every afternoon to keep her from following through?

    A. Daniel threatens her daily. B. She sees Daniel and fears him.   C. She is kept too busy.

11. True or False: Andi plans to tell Melinda her secret during their Saturday ride.

12. What outrageous request does Daniel ask of the girls? _____

    _____

13. Why is Andi riding so closely to the edge of the deep gully? _____

    _____

14. Why doesn't Andi jump off Taffy when Melinda yells at her to jump? _____

    _____

THE LAST RIDE: VOCABULARY-LEARNING MEANINGS FROM CONTEXT

For each underlined word below, circle the closest definition for its meaning. Then use the word in a sentence of your own.

1. Justin had tried to find their sister all those years ago, but to no avail.

   without limits   (without success)   without improvement   without happiness

   She tried to make the recipe turn out, but to no avail.

2. It appeared Justin had scoured all the places where a youth could find trouble.

   searched   scrubbed   rubbed   listed

   _____

3. Daniel appeared subdued at last.

   hushed   serious   happy   submissive

   _____

4. No respectable person knew anything about the vile pastime of cockfighting.

   dangerous   interesting   disgusting   entertaining

   _____

5. Remorse that Andi had accused Johnny for the thefts washed over her.

   guilt   anger   joy   disgust

   _____

6. The town could revel in its gossip, but no one would ever suspect a Carter of theft.

   yell   mourn   take pleasure   gather

   _____

7. For all his surliness, Andi never thought Daniel would actually strike her.

   friendliness   wavering   indecisiveness   hostility

   _____

8. How would Daniel retaliate if Andi and Melinda abandoned him in the hills?

   behave   get even   get home   feel

   _____

9. "You can stay and pamper Daniel if you want to," Melinda told Andi. "I'm going home."

   baby   visit with   argue with   look for

   _____

THE LAST RIDE: GIANTS IN THE LAND!

At the beginning of chapter seventeen, Andi is scared. As much as she would like to tell somebody about Daniel's secret thefts, she's too frightened at what he might do. She compares herself to the **Israelites**, who wanted to enter the Promised Land but were too frightened of the "giants" to follow through.

The account of the Israelites' failure to take the land is recorded in **Numbers** 13 and 14. This is an astonishing account, considering it was the people already dwelling in the land who were, in reality, scared to death of the people of God. **Forty** years later, when **Joshua** led the people across the Jordan, a couple of spies in Jericho heard it for themselves: "I know the Lord has given you the land, and that the terror of you has fallen on us. For we have heard how the Lord dried up the Red Sea before you [forty years ago, and they still remember!] when you came out of Egypt. When we heard it, our hearts melted, and no courage remained" (Joshua 2: 9–11).

If only the spies Moses had sent out forty years earlier to spy out Canaan had heard such words. One man from each of the twelve tribes was chosen as part of the delegation to check out the land. Was it a rich land? A mighty people? Weaknesses? Fortified cities or open cities? In other words, bring back word so we'll know how to conquer it. They spent forty days doing their job thoroughly. They even cut huge branches of grapes. This place was a paradise!

The people eagerly awaited the spies' **report**. After all, they'd left **Egypt** two years before and no doubt eagerly looked forward to finally entering what four hundred years before had been their own land, the land God had originally given to Abraham and all his descendants (Genesis 15:18).

Imagine the wailing and disappointment when the **spies** gave their report: It's a grand land, flowing with "**milk and honey**" (an idiom for richness). But there's one slight problem: the men of this land are huge (**giants**). And strong. Their cities are like fortresses. "We became like **grasshoppers** [a simile] in our own sight, and so we were in their sight" (Num. 13:33).

The Israelites cross the Jordan River

Two of the spies, Joshua and Caleb, recognized the danger. After all, that's what they had been sent into the land to do—scout it out. But **Caleb** insisted they could take the land. "Do not fear the people of the land, for they will be our prey" (Numbers 14:9). But ten of the spies felt like Andi. They were overcome with fear (clearly forgetting the whole Red Sea event and the destruction of Pharaoh's army). They gave a bad report to the people, and the unofficial "vote" went out: "Let's find ourselves a new leader and hightail it back to Egypt!"

Moses, God's chosen leader over His people, was appalled at the people's uproar (all two million of them). He fell on his face before the congregation. Joshua and Caleb tore their clothes and pleaded with the people to trust God. The people were so discouraged and terrified that they threatened to stone the two spies to shut them up. (How dare they tell us to trust God when things look bad!)

God was not exactly happy, either. He'd had enough of these rebellious people and told Moses He would strike them with a plague and make a great nation out of Moses instead. Moses begged God for the lives of the people, and the Lord repented (changed His mind) about wiping them out. Instead, He gave them a punishment to fit their crime of unbelief: They would wander around in the wilderness one year for each day the spies had scouted the land: forty years.

After forty years, the Israelites who had not died of old age had learned their lesson. They followed Joshua without hesitation and proceeded to conquer the land. I bet they were surprised to see how the people of Canaan had been watching and waiting and trembling in fear for all of those forty years.

WORD SEARCH

Use the clues to find 12 words that have to do with giants in the land. Words can be across, down, diagonal, forward, or backward: (the 12 words are clues in **BOLD** on these two pages)

R	B	X	R	B	E	L	A	C	A	X	U	E	S	T
Q	F	R	G	E	G	F	Y	S	C	X	S	E	J	P
S	D	A	S	T	X	I	M	J	Y	B	T	X	O	Y
Y	E	N	O	H	D	N	A	K	L	I	M	S	S	G
Z	Z	S	P	Q	R	P	W	N	L	D	E	R	H	E
S	Q	H	O	E	L	G	Y	E	T	I	V	E	U	P
P	V	P	P	M	F	K	A	O	P	S	X	P	A	Z
H	F	O	R	T	Y	R	X	S	O	J	E	P	A	A
U	R	Q	R	D	S	R	X	O	C	F	B	O	Z	M
T	V	Y	M	I	U	R	P	B	L	S	O	H	J	G
I	X	D	W	B	H	K	X	O	C	E	G	S	V	U
E	N	N	M	Z	V	V	Z	G	V	K	U	S	N	A
J	R	T	C	B	A	P	X	N	A	T	L	A	O	Q
I	X	V	Z	N	U	M	B	E	R	S	W	R	M	M
D	L	Z	R	V	V	V	Q	S	C	J	V	G	R	R

1. the leader of God's people

2. the number of years spend wandering in the wilderness

3. Moses sent_____ to look at the land.

4. Ten brought back a bad _____

5. & 6. the names of two of the spies

7. the book in the Bible that records this account of spying out the land

8. ten spies brought back reports of these huge people

9. the land Moses led the people out of

10. God's people are called _____ 11. The people felt like_____next to the people of the land.

12. a name that describes the richness of the Promised Land (three words; no spaces between the words)

The Last Ride: Chapters 18–21

CHAPTERS 18–19

1. Chapter 18 is the only chapter in the book without a journal entry. Why do you think there is no entry for this chapter? _____

2. Circle the four people who join Andi and Melinda at the bottom of the draw:

   Mother • Justin • Chad • Mitch • Daniel • Dr. Weaver

3. Which two from the list above are not at the gully? Explain why they are not there.

   _____-_____

   _____-_____

4. List Andi's injuries: _____ _____

   _____ _____

5. What promise does Andi want to hear from Chad? _____

6. Who jumps in and makes a promise of his own? _____

7. Why do you think Dr. Weaver doesn't want Mother to tell Andi the extent of Taffy's injuries?

   _____

   _____

CHAPTERS 20–21

8. Why are Uncle Benjamin and Aunt Lydia proud of Daniel? _____

   _____

9. What does Andi want to do right after supper? _____

10. Who breaks the awful news to Andi that Taffy had to be put down? _____

11. True or False: Andi thinks Mitch's promise to not let Chad shoot Taffy was nothing more than a mean trick to lead her to believe her mare would not be shot.

12. When Benjamin and Lydia go back to New York, Daniel will not be with them. Why not?

   _____

13. What book is Andi absorbed in reading? _____

14. Andi knows deep inside she's hurting her family, but she is far from healing at this point. What words does she use to describe herself? _____

15. True or false? Andi gives Riley permission to drop the "Miss Carter" nonsense.

THE LAST RIDE: VOCABULARY-LEARNING MEANINGS FROM CONTEXT

For each of the underlined words below, write a definition in your own words. Use an online dictionary for help if needed. (See example.)

1. Deep <u>lacerations</u> crusted with dirt traversed Taffy's flank and rump.

   "lacerations" are . . . <u>   deep cuts; scratches   </u>

2. Andi lay in the dim world between awareness and <u>oblivion</u>.

   "oblivion" means . . . _____

3. The sun had dropped behind the gully's sides, but the air was still <u>stifling</u>.

   "stifling" means . . . _____

4. "Taffy will need a <u>travois</u>," Andi said.

   "a travois" is . . . _____

5. A sliver of doubt about Taffy's well-being threatened to shatter Andi's <u>optimism</u>.

   "optimism" means . . . _____

6. Mother <u>enfolded</u> Andi's good hand in her own.

   "enfolded" means . . . _____

7. In spite of Andi's resolve to get well soon, she found herself <u>confined</u> to bed a long time.

   "confined" means . . . _____

8. The wheelchair included the added luxury of a <u>chamber pot</u>.

   "a chamber pot" is . . . _____

9. It was doubly <u>mortifying</u> for strangers to see her helpless and trussed up like a mummy.

   "mortifying" means . . . _____

10. Baby Sammy banged his spoon on his highchair tray and <u>squalled</u> for his supper.

    "squalled" means . . . _____

11. Andi's heart closed tight against the <u>despicable</u> young man.

    "despicable" means . . . _____

12. Andi stroked the dog's head, <u>suppressing</u> a smile.

    "suppressing" means . . . _____

13. The dime novel had terrified Andi as much as it had <u>captivated</u> her as a little girl.

    "captivated" means . . . _____

The Last Ride: A Journey to the Centre of the Earth

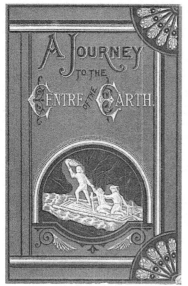

When chapter 21 opens, Andi is reading a book Justin dropped by for her, hoping to spark her interest. It does! *A Journey to the Centre of the Earth* is a science fiction novel written by Jules Verne and first published in French in 1864 (Andi read the 1871 English version). The story revolves around a German professor, Otto Lidenbrock, who believes there are volcanic tubes going down toward the center of the Earth. He cracks a secret code to find the entrance through a certain crater in an Icelandic volcano. He, his non-adventurous nephew Axel, and their guide, Hans, descend into the earth and encounter many dangerous adventures: an underground ocean, prehistoric animals, and even giant humans. They eventually return to the surface through a vent in the Stromboli volcano in Italy. The professor is hailed as a great, scientific genius for discovering so many new wonders.

Through the years, millions of readers have thrilled to Jules Verne's astonishing imagination. To download and read a copy of this exciting book for yourself, go here. Most of the early classics are in public domain and free for the taking.

http://manybooks.net/titles/vernejul1885718857-8.html#

WEB FUN: Many movie versions of *A Journey to the Centre of the Earth* have been produced. Copy this link into your browser and watch the official movie trailer for the 1959 version starring Pat Boone. **https://www.youtube.com/watch?v=0v7FtXNuQlY** (This is a great movie, by the way.)

Besides *A Journey to the Center of the Earth*, Jules Verne wrote other books with which you may or may not be familiar: *Five Weeks in a Balloon, Twenty Thousand Leagues Under the Sea, The Mysterious Island, From the Earth to the Moon*, and *Around the World in Eighty Days*. Some of his scientific ideas about outer space and undersea exploration in the 1800s seemed outrageously unbelievable at the time. However, today we have traveled to the moon and under the sea in quite a similar manner as he wrote.

Jules Verne is considered one of the foremost authors responsible for launching the science fiction genre of novels, along with H.G. Wells (*The Time Machine* and *War of the Worlds*). Unfortunately, his masterful works lost quite a bit when translated into English. The American and British publishers also marketed the books to a younger audience, which hurt Jules Verne's reputation by limiting him as a "children's" author in most English-speaking countries.

THE LAST RIDE: THE FIVE ELEMENTS OF A FICTION STORY

A good fiction story includes these five essential elements: interesting CHARACTERS, a creative SETTING, an intriguing STORY PROBLEM, exciting PLOT EVENTS, and a satisfying STORY RESOLUTION. Jules Verne created excellent stories using these elements. Let's explore the five story elements for *A Journey to the Centre of the Earth*.

1. CHARACTERS

Professor Otto Lidenbrock: a man of science and astonishing impatience

Axel: Professor Lidenbrock's nephew; a cautious and unadventurous student

Hans Bjelke: an Icelander who becomes their guide

Grauben: Professor Lidenbrock's goddaughter, with whom Axel is in love

2. SETTING

Germany, Iceland, under the earth, an underground ocean, volcanoes, Italy

3. STORY PROBLEM

Professor Lidenbrock must crack a code to discover a secret way into the bowels of the earth so he can explore what no man has ever seen before.

4. PLOT EVENTS

Lidenbrock finds the runes in code and deciphers them; he and Axel go to Iceland, hire a guide, and find the secret entrance into the crater; Axel tries to talk his uncle out of descending; they run out of water; they tap into an underground stream and encounter an ocean; they narrowly avoid colossal monsters; they discover a beach full of bones; the sea rushes into a seemingly bottomless pit; their raft gets swept up into a volcanic vent; they come out in Italy

5. STORY RESOLUTION

Professor Lidenbrock and Axel return to Hamburg, Germany, where the professor is hailed as a great scientist. He has accomplished what he set out to do. Axel marries his sweetheart, Grauben, and Hans returns to Iceland, none the worse for wear.

IT'S YOUR TURN

On the next page, use what you have learned about the five elements of a fiction story by filling out the information asked for regarding the novel, *The Last Ride*. The page is too limited to include every character or every plot event in the book, but remember what you can. Also, for the story ending, write how you think it will end (unless you have read ahead and know).

The Last Ride

Susan K. Marlow

THE FIVE ELEMENTS OF *THE LAST RIDE*

1. CHARACTERS

_____

_____

_____

_____

_____

2. SETTING

_____

3. STORY PROBLEM

_____

_____

_____

_____

4. PLOT EVENTS

_____

_____

_____

_____

_____

_____

_____

5. STORY RESOLUTION

_____

_____

_____

_____

The Last Ride: Chapters 22–26

CHAPTERS 22–24

1. What is Riley Prescott's "jim-dandy" idea? _____

_____

2. Riley says, "That fall took part of your family down with you, didn't it?" None of the other Carters actually fell down into the gully. Riley is speaking figuratively. What does he mean?

_____

3. Riley has taught Shasta a trick that shocks Andi and makes her gasp. What trick is it?

   A. He stands up on his hind legs.   B. He bows on command. C. He counts with his hooves.

4. Name two things Shasta does to show Andi he misses her and doesn't like her absence:

_____   _____

5. After Riley says his "piece," Andi bursts into tears. Why do you think she does this?

_____

6. How long has it been since Andi's accident? _____

7. What happens on "graduation day"? _____

8. Why will Andi be sore after riding today? _____

CHAPTERS 25–26

9. Where has Riley brought Andi? _____

10. Andi asks, "Why have you brought me here?" What is Riley's answer? _____

_____

11. True or false? Andi "fires" Riley on the spot for talking to her in such a manner.

12. Why can't Andi leave? _____

13. What is the name of the horse Riley owned as a child? _____

14. Why is Andi moved by Riley's story? _____

15. How does she respond (two ways)? _____

_____

16. What awaits Andi at home? _____

17. Why do you think Andi is glad that Riley is not her brother? _____

THE LAST RIDE: VOCABULARY-SYNONYMS AND ANTONYMS

Synonyms are words that have the same (or nearly the same) meaning as the original word. Write the **synonym** for each underlined word on the line to the right.

Antonyms are words that mean the opposite. Below each sentence are four words. One of the words is the **antonym.** Circle the antonym for each underlined word.

1. Andi felt like a <u>prissy</u> old lady.   <u>   prim & proper   </u>

    sick & weak   (*casual*)   *prim & proper*   *sad*

2. Andi stiffened and <u>clammed up</u>.   _____

    shut her mouth   *listened*   *slept*   *talked a lot*

3. "I've just <u>acquired</u> another brother," Andi told herself.   _____

    purchased   *lost*   *seen*   *gained*

4. *Not that I have any place special to go,* Andi mused <u>sourly</u>.   _____

    quietly   *bitterly*   *agreeably*   *unknowingly*

5. Riley <u>cajoled</u> Andi into watching him work with the colts.   _____

    sweet-talked   *forced*   *lured*   *tickled*

6. The <u>staccato</u> of approaching hoof beats urged Andi faster.   _____

    loud sounds   *blurred sounds*   *happy sounds*   *clipped sounds*

7. Shasta slowed in response to Andi's <u>nonverbal</u> command.   _____

    shouted   *pleading*   *urgent*   *unspoken*

8. "You won't feel fine tomorrow," Riley said <u>ominously</u>.   _____

    sadly   *encouragingly*   *jokingly*   *threateningly*

9. Andi never wanted to see the <u>disreputable</u> young man again.   _____

    disgraceful   *mean*   *honorable*   *shoddy*

10. Sid McCoy often <u>berated</u> Andi for one thing or another.   _____

    praised   *teased*   *loved*   *criticized*

11. Andi laughed at Riley's <u>antics</u>.   _____

    adventures   *clowning*   *seriousness*   *laziness*

12. It took all of Andi's <u>resolve</u> to look at the rocky mound.   _____

    weakness   *character*   *determination*   *honor*

THE LAST RIDE: SCRIPTURE MINI-POSTERS

Andi loves horses! The Bible mentions horses numerous times. Here are a few verses. Look them up and choose two that spark your interest. Copy them onto the cards below and cut them out. Job 39:19–20; Psalm 20:7; Proverbs 21:31; Habakkuk 1:8; Revelation 19:11

THE LAST RIDE: NEW YORK CITY TRAVEL TRIVIA

What would Andi see if she visited New York City? Use the Internet to explore these important New York City landmarks. Fill in the facts, then write "YES" or "NO" in the box if the landmark is something Daniel could show Andi in 1884 (if he ever gets out of jail).

1. St. Patrick's Cathedral

2. Statue of Liberty

3. Empire State Building

1. Year it opened: _____

Catholic or Protestant church? (circle your answer)

2. Year it opened:_____

Construction began in what year? _____

3. Year it opened: _____

How many stories high is the Empire State Bldg.? _____

4. Central Park

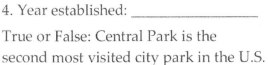

4. Year established: _____

True or False: Central Park is the second most visited city park in the U.S.

5. Flatiron Building

5. Year it opened: _____

The real name of this triangular-shaped building is the _____ Building.

It was named "Flatiron Building" because it looks like an _____.

Daily Schedule for Book 4: Courageous Love

*indicates an optional activity found in the *Circle C Milestones* lapbook.

(Lapbook activities can be skipped or purchased from CircleCAdventures.com)

	Day 1	**Day 2**	**Day 3**	**Day 4**
Courageous Love	Chapters 1-2	Chapters 3	Chapters 4-5	— — — — —
Literature Guide	Page 113	Page 115 #1-9	Page 115 #10-16	* *Lapbook activity for chapters 1-5*
	Day 5	**Day 6**	**Day 7**	**Day 8**
Courageous Love	— — — — —	— — — — —	Chapters 6-7	Chapters 8-9
Literature Guide	Pages 116-118	Pages 119-121	Page 122 #1-7	Page 122 #8-12
	Day 9	**Day 10**	**Day 11**	**Day 12**
Courageous Love	— — — — —	— — — — —	Chapter 10	Chapter 11
Literature Guide	* *Lapbook activities (2) for chapters 6-9*	Pages 123-124	Pages 125-126	Page 127 #1-7
	Day 13	**Day 14**	**Day 15**	**Day 16**
Courageous Love	Chapters 12-13	— — — — —	— — — — —	— — — — —
Literature Guide	Page 127 #8-16	* *Lapbook activity for chapters 10-13*	Pages 128-129	Pages 130-131
	Day 17	**Day 18**	**Day 19**	**Day 20**
Courageous Love	Chapters 14-15	Chapters 16-17	— — — — —	— — — — —
Literature Guide	Page 132 #1-8	Page 132 #9-13	* *Lapbook activity for chapters 14-17*	Pages 133-135
	Day 21	**Day 22**	**Day 23**	**Day 24**
Courageous Love	Chapters 18-19	Chapters 20-21	— — — — —	— — — — —
Literature Guide	Page 136 # 1-7	Page 136 #8-15	* *Lapbook activity for chapters 18-21*	Pages 137-139
	Day 25	**Day 26**	**Day 27**	**Day 28**
Courageous Love	Chapters 22-24	Chapters 25-26	— — — — —	— — — — —
Literature Guide	Page 140 #1-9	Page 140 #10-17	* *Lapbook activity for chapters 22-26*	Pages 141-144

Story Synopsis: Andi is turning seventeen when *Courageous Love* opens. Nothing gives her greater joy than knowing she can pull her own weight on the ranch. She spends her free time learning to trick ride on Shasta under the watchful eye of Riley Prescott, the Circle C's wrangler. Andi's oldest brother, Justin, is married and has a toddler. Brother Mitch has gone off to cow college in Berkeley, her sister Melinda is married, and Chad is next in line. While heading home to get ready for Chad's engagement party in town, Riley and Andi stumble on a mystery: Why has the fence surrounding Mitch's special breed of heifers been cut? And that's just the beginning of their woes. When evidence points to revenge-seeking escaped prisoners Justin prosecuted years ago for robbery and murder, none of the Carters feel safe. Andi must summon all her courage for the horrifying experiences that lie ahead for her, her sister-in-law Lucy, and her little nephew Sammy. The character theme for *Courageous Love* is "courage." In your best handwriting, copy Joshua 1:9 from page 3 in the book. Color, cut out the poster, and memorize this verse during your study.

COURAGE:

COURAGE IS BEING SCARED TO DEATH . . . BUT SADDLING UP ANYWAY

Courageous Love: Chapters 1–5

CHAPTERS 1–3

1. What is Andi doing when the story opens? _____

2. Andi is not alone. Who is with her? _____ What is his role?

_____

3. Circle the reasons Riley refuses to teach Andi the somersault trick.

    He doesn't have time. • It's too dangerous. • Her skirt can easily get caught.

    Andi is not tall enough.   •   The timing has to be just right.   •   The falls are too bad.

4. Name the injuries Andi got falling off Dakota. _____ _____

5. Why is she so upset about it? _____

_____

6. Where is Mitch these days? _____

7. To the right is a drawing of barbed wire. What is wrong with the barbed-wire fence Andi and

    Riley check out? _____

8. What is Andi's favorite ranch task?

    A. counting cattle   B. mucking out stalls   C. lassoing   D. branding calves

9. Andi quotes part of Psalm 91:11 to Riley. Look up and copy the entire verse.

_____

_____

_____

CHAPTERS 4–5

10. Chad's fiancée is the new teacher. What is her name? _____

11. Instead of dancing, Andi decides to visit with which Carter? _____

12. Why does Andi agree to dance with Oliver Jansen? _____

_____

13. Who comes to Andi's rescue? A. Mitch   B. Cory   C. Levi   D. Justin   E. Johnny Wilson

14. What does he say that shocks and upsets Andi? _____

15. How does Andi's dress get ruined? _____

16. Andi is alone with baby Samuel when something terrible happens? What is it?

_____

From the first time she watched eight-year-old Riley stand up on his black horse, Midnight, Andi has wanted to learn to trick ride. Her desire was reinforced when she saw the cowhand Toledo do a somersault, fly off his horse, and land on his feet (with his hat still on his head). Ever since then, Andi has itched to try a similar riding stunt for herself. But ranch boss Chad insists a working ranch is no place for such foolishness. Besides, he believes it's downright dangerous.

What is trick riding? It is the act of performing stunts on horseback. Andi is familiar with standing on Shasta while galloping. She knows about the somersault trick. Riley also teaches Andi the pickup trick. There are many other kinds of riding stunts. Here are a few:

THE DEATH DRAG

❖   Using a strap, the rider hangs upside down off the side of a horse while galloping around the arena (death drag).

❖   The rider runs and jumps onto a galloping horse, and then jumps off the horse.

❖   While galloping, the rider crawls under the belly of his/her horse and back into the saddle.

❖   The rider hangs lengthwise along the side of a galloping horse (Apache hideaway). The native Americans used this trick to avoid being wounded during battle.

❖   In Roman riding, the rider stands atop a pair of cantering horses with one foot on each horse. This stunt goes back to the time of the Roman Empire. Sometimes this stunt includes five horses with the rider standing atop the inner three horses.

Trick riding is relatively new to America. Earlier in history, Russian Cossacks rode like crazy, performing tricks on their horses to evade their enemies. Soon, Americans caught on to these eye-popping stunts. In the late 1800s, cowboys competed for prize money at rodeos and Wild West shows. However, trick-riding rodeo competitions came to an end in the 1940s. Why? Chad was right. Trick riding is dangerous. Performers were taking too many chances to earn the prize. Today, stunt riding is a specialty act and not a competition at rodeos, fairs, or other events.

VAULTING

Vaulting is another type of stunt riding that involves gymnastics on horseback. Vaulting is considered a competitive sport. It has a long history of being an equestrian circus act, but its origins really trace back two thousand years to the Roman games. Another origin is ancient Crete, where people performed acrobatic moves around wild bulls. Beginning vaulters compete at a walk or a trot while experienced vaulters canter. They perform routines to music and must include a certain number of movements in their act.

Andi's Favorite Riding Stunt

Based on what you have read about trick riding and vaulting, use the clues to fill in the words in this double puzzle. When you are finished, use the numbered letters to discover Andi's favorite riding stunt. This stunt comes in handy near the end of *Courageous Love*.

1. A competitive riding sport.

☐ ☐ ☐ ☐ ☐ ☐ ☐
     8   1   5

2. This stunt requires you to crawl under a horse's _____.

☐ ☐ ☐ ☐ ☐
    3

3. Take a leap, turn a _____, then land on your feet next to your horse's head.

☐ ☐ ☐ ☐ ☐ ☐ ☐ ☐ ☐ ☐
   3   4   8

4. A possible place of origin for the sport of vaulting.

☐ ☐ ☐ ☐
6 4 3   3

5. Riley teaches Andi this trick first.

☐ ☐ ☐ ☐ ☐ ☐
1   8 2

6. You need more than one horse for this.

☐ ☐ ☐ ☐   ☐ ☐ ☐ ☐ ☐
4   4   5

7. You need this while performing the death drag.

☐ ☐ ☐ ☐ ☐
1   2

8. Riding stunts are also called riding _____.

☐ ☐ ☐ ☐ ☐ ☐
1   7

Andi's Favorite Stunt Is . . .

☐ H ☐   ☐ ☐ ☐ ☐ ☐ ☐   ☐ ☐ ☐ ☐ ☐
1   3   2 5 6 7 8 2   1 4 5 6 7

Web Fun

Fourteen-year-old sisters Bethany and Brittany, along with their ten-year-old sister Libby, show the *Kansas City Star* their Roman riding and "suicide drag" (death drag). Copy the address into your web browser to watch their stunts. **www.youtube.com/watch?v=ZBG-KhSyVgQ**

COURAGEOUS LOVE: UNIVERSITY OF CALIFORNIA, BERKELEY

UC Berkeley fifteen years after Mitch attended (1900), with the Golden Gate in the background (the bridge came later)

In the fall of 1884, Mitch Carter enrolls in the University of California at Berkeley. Although he has ranched all his life, Mitch wants to expand his agricultural knowledge. The cow college (as Chad jokingly calls it) can teach him new ways to approach agriculture. In later chapters, Mitch's new knowledge helps his heifers.

In 1868, when Mitch was ten years old, a private California college merged with the Agriculture, Mining, and Mechanical Arts College in Oakland to become the University of California. Five years later in 1873, the university moved to its Berkeley campus. That first year 167 male students and twenty-two female students were enrolled. It was the first full-curriculum public university in the state of California.

Because the Agricultural, Mining, and Mechanical Arts College had previously taken advantage of a federal land-grant-to-colleges act, all male students were required to serve two hours a week (for four years) in a military capacity. They were trained in tactics, military drills, marksmanship, camp duty, and fortifications. One of the campus halls, North Hall, housed an armory. In 1904, this requirement was reduced to two years of service. It eventually became the military's "Reserve Officers' Training Corps (ROTC) that many colleges offer today.

THINK IT THROUGH

What would you like to do after you complete your elementary, middle, and high school education? Is college on your radar? On the lines below, list two interests. Next to your interests, write what (if anything) you need to do to make your interests become a reality.

_____	_____
_____	_____

SNIPPETS FROM ANDI'S JOURNAL

Mother and Melinda hint about my becoming a teacher, but honestly! All my life I have wanted to be a rancher and horse trainer. Even though Chad and I clash a lot, he is the best rancher in California, and hence my best teacher. Lately, however, I've been thinking hard. When I'm with Baby Samuel, I think it would be mighty fun to raise babies too. I wonder if I can do both?

Courageous Love: Making Future Plans-Bible Bookmark

It's exciting to think about all the things that await you as you grow and mature. However, as you think about your future, make sure you continually consult the Lord. Below are five Bible verses about making plans. Choose one that speaks to you especially and cut it out on the dotted lines.

Call to Me, and I will answer you, and show you great and mighty things, which you do not know. *Jeremiah 33:3*

A man's heart plans his way but the LORD directs his steps Proverbs 16:9

For I know the thoughts that I think toward you, says the LORD, thoughts of peace and not of evil, to give you a future and a hope. Jeremiah 29:11

He has shown you, O man, what is good; and what does the LORD require of you but to do justly, to love mercy, and to walk humbly with your God? Micah 6:8

There are many plans in a man's heart, nevertheless the LORD's counsel—that will stand. Proverbs 19:21

Glue the verse inside the border on the bookmark below.* Color and cut it out. Glue to light cardstock and then laminate. Punch a hole where shown and tie a thin satin ribbon through it. Keep the bookmark in your Bible to refer to when planning your future. Or give it to a friend or family member.

*Hint: Make copies of this page if you want to make more than one bookmark so you can use the other verses.

Courageous Love: Vocabulary & Grammar

For each underlined word below, write the part of speech (noun, verb, or adjective) on the line. Then choose the best definition for how the word is used in the sentence. (See example.)

1. Andi better not take a tumble while <u>disregarding</u> Riley's instructions. _____VERB_____

    A. following   (B. ignoring)   C. heeding   D. imitating

2. The promise Andi gave Chad to never practice a stunt alone <u>rankled</u> her. _____

    A. irritated   B. pleased   C. soothed   D. excited

3. Andi ducked her head, <u>chagrined</u>. She had not seen the danger. _____

    A. unhappy   B. annoyed   C. angry   D. saddened

4. "A different bull might get in. That would <u>aggravate</u> Mitch." _____

    A. make him happy   B. surprise   C. exasperate   D. mollify

5. "Why don't you <u>tally</u> the heifers while I piece this fence back together?" _____

    A. count   B. round up   C. brand   D. check

6. "The day's a-wastin'. We don't want to be late for Chad's <u>shindig</u>." _____

    A. speech   B. wedding   C. party   D. instructions

7. Riley's <u>wry</u> remark brought Andi back from the brink of worry.

    A. unkind   B. loving   C. bored   D. amused

8. Aunt Rebecca's <u>drivel</u> echoed in Andi's head. _____

    A. laugh   B. nonsense   C. scolding   D. wisdom

9. "Even partially <u>reformed</u>, Johnny still can get under your skin." _____

    A. forgiven   B. matured   C. improved   D. scolded

Snippets from Andi's Journal

Ever since I was six years old, Johnny Wilson has acted worse than a plague of locusts toward me. But I have to admit I was grateful to him for spilling coffee down my new party dress at Chad's gala the other night. Because of my ruined dress, I was able to sneak away and find a corner. Thanks, Johnny!

Courageous Love: Chapters 6–9

CHAPTERS 6–7

1. This is an illustration of where Andi goes to protect Sammy. What is it called? _____

2. What do we call this type of furniture today? _____

3. Why is Andi worried that Aunt Rebecca might have heard the crash of breaking glass?

   _____

4. Three men keep the curious crowd away from the injured and hurry them out the door. Who are they? _____   _____   _____

5. What is the cryptic message written on the piece of leather tied around the brick?

   _____

6. Riley believes the note refers to the fence being cut. Do you agree? What do *you* think has happened to Mitch's heifers? _____

   _____

7. Andi stays behind when the men go out to the herd. Who goes along instead? _____

CHAPTERS 8–9

8. True or false? Andi quietly pads down the stairs and slips outside because Mother has not given her permission to go out to Mitch's Angus herd.

9. How many dead heifers does Andi find? _____

10. What is the cause of their death? _____

11. Alkali is a white powder also called _____ and can be found in your kitchen cupboard.

12. Fifteen members of the extended Carter family crowd around the table for Sunday dinner. Can you place them in their correct seats based on the clues? (Use initials to save space.)

- ~~Justin sits at one end; Elizabeth sits at the other end.~~
- Sammy sits in a high chair between Justin and Lucy.
- Rebecca sits on the other side of Justin.
- Andi sits between Rebecca and Betsy. Levi sits by Betsy.
- Melinda sits between Lucy and her husband, Peter.
- Kate sits by Hannah and also by Elizabeth.
- Mitch sits by Elizabeth. Chad's fiancée Ellie sits between Chad and Mitch.

COURAGEOUS LOVE: VOCABULARY-MATCHING

Match the underlined word in each phrase with the correct meaning. Page numbers where the word is first used are given so you can find the meaning using the context of the sentence. The first one has been done for you.

SECTION A: CHAPTERS 6–7:

1. __D__ she crooned to her baby (p. 45)

2. _____ a quiet oasis (p. 47)

3. _____ to gawk at the injured (p. 47)

4. _____ to scrutinize someone (p. 48)

5. _____ to rummage through a trunk (p. 51)

6. _____ eyes round with misgiving (p. 56)

7. _____ to mingle with the crowd (p. 58)

8. _____ a pristine stock tank (p. 59)

9. _____ to escalate into a problem (p. 67)

10. _____ an idea has merit (p. 68)

A. value; worth

B. refuge; sanctuary

C. search; dig around

D. ~~spoke in a soft, gentle manner~~

E. unspoiled; unsullied

F. mix in; blend

G. worry; doubt

H. inspect or examine closely

I. stare rudely; gape

J. intensify; get worse

DIGGING DEEPER

The age-old whine "It's not fair!" nearly bursts from Andi's lips when she finds out she can't go along with her brothers to check on the calves. She gives in, but not happily. Describe a time when you felt as if something was not quite fair in your family. How did you react? How did it turn out? How could Philippians 2:4 help you have a better mindset the next time things are not fair?

_____

_____

_____

_____

_____

_____

_____

Courageous Love: Wind Pumps

A wind pump and livestock tank

Windmills have been around ever since people figured out how to harness the wind's energy for various purposes. A windmill can be used to grind grain, pump water, or create electricity.

The windmill on the Circle C ranch is actually called a wind pump. It is used exclusively for bringing up water from an underground well for livestock to drink. Daniel Hallady invented this type of wind pump in 1854, and its use quickly spread all across rural America.

How Does a Wind Pump Work?

The top part of the wind pump turns freely so it can catch the wind no matter which direction it blows. On a breezy day, the vanes spin continuously. The blade apparatus connects to a set of gears that makes a rod go up and down. This long rod extends deep underground and is attached to a pump inside the well. Cylinders with pistons and one-way flaps allow the water to be pulled to the surface and discharged into a holding tank without falling back into the well. WEB FUN: This 1:30 minute YouTube video shows a wind pump in action. Carefully copy this address into your web browser and enjoy. **www.youtube.com/watch?v=iHvgpMnyfVk**

Acid and Alkali

Andi's brothers drain the stock tank to flush out the alkali that has poisoned Mitch's heifers. To show how dangerous a high concentration of alkali in the water is to cattle, do this experiment. What happens when ACID (like inside a cow's stomach) combines with ALKALI (baking soda)?

Supplies: • 2 tablespoons baking soda   • 1/2 cup water   • 1/2 cup vinegar   • large glass bowl

Mix the baking soda and water until it dissolves. Pour into a large glass bowl. Slowly add part of the vinegar to the soda water. What happens? _____

When the reaction stops, add more vinegar. What keeps happening? _____

What does this experiment show about what happens when a cow drinks water with a high concentration of alkali? _____

The reaction that occurs inside the cow's acidic stomach has devastating results. The gas bubbles created by the chemical reaction cause the cow to bloat and to belch. This can bring up the stomach contents, which burn the throat and can also seep into the cow's airway. If it is not caught early enough, death follows. Pouring grease down the cow's throat coats the lining of the throat and helps prevent the acid burns.

COURAGEOUS LOVE: BARBED WIRE

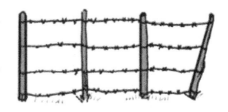

Andi yanked at the wire with all her might to give Riley the slack he needed to overlap the two cut ends. Even through the leather protection, Andi felt the pinprick of barbs. She moved her hands slightly to avoid the sharp points.

"Pinprick" is too gentle a word to describe being jabbed by barbed wire. It scratches worse than a cat's claws—more like a cougar! Barbed wire comes in huge rolls that can weigh up to fifty pounds. If you lose control while handling this type of fencing, the wire will twang and snap and can wrap itself around your body. It can also dig deeply into your flesh. It pays to be careful when stringing barbed wire.

This is a close-up of a barb. A machine twists them into place along a length of wire fencing. This type of fencing is quite effective in keeping livestock enclosed. It is inexpensive and simple to put up. It only requires posts (wooden or metal), the barbed wire, and staples or wire attachments. In the 1800s, many posts were cut from young pine trees of the proper diameter.

Before the Civil War, the West was wide open. Livestock moved freely, with all ranchers' cattle mingling. They were rounded up and separated a couple times a year. After the war, with more settlers moving west, ranchers needed to set boundaries. Other types of fencing were horribly expensive or not available (like the rock walls and hedges back East). Farmers in the Fresno area spent $4,000 ($75,000 in today's dollars) on lumber to erect wooden fences to protect 2,500 acres of wheat from free-ranging livestock. A cheaper method to keep cattle contained was needed.

In the 1860s, Joseph Glidden wanted to invent a durable wire fence with fixed barbs (smooth wire fences did not keep the cattle contained). He and a friend used a grindstone to twist two wires together to hold sharp barbs in place. The invention was a hit, and the first patent was issued in 1867. One fan wrote, "It takes no room, exhausts no soil, shades no vegetation, is proof against high winds, makes no snowdrifts, and is both durable and cheap."

That fan summed up barbed wire well. It is still the most popular wire fencing today. Cattle and other livestock respect it. Their thick hides prevent serious injury from brushing up against the barbs. It is not the best fencing for horses, however. They can be injured much more easily with barbed wire than cattle, sometimes becoming entangled in a broken fence (from thrashing against the pain). In that rare case, there is little that can be done to extract the horse until it has exhausted itself. Humans can also be seriously injured while working with barbed wire. However, proper clothing and slow, careful movements can prevent the sharp, stinging "bites" of barbed wire.

COURAGEOUS LOVE: BARBED WIRE CROSSWORD PUZZLE

Everything in this puzzle has to do with barbed wire. Use the clues below to navigate your way through this prickly barbed-wire crossword puzzle.

ACROSS

2. The prickly part of barbed wire.

6. The inventor of barbed wire.

7. The number of wires needed to twist the barbs in place.

8. Farmers here spent $4,000 to build a wood fence around their wheat fields.

9. This is issued to an inventor.

10. Barbed wire scratches worse than a _____.

11. In the 1800s, fence posts were cut from these.

DOWN

1. These animals have thick hides to protect them from barbed wire.

3. The weight of a roll of barbed wire in pounds.

4. Most livestock _____ barbed wire.

5. These animals do not react well to barbed wire.

6. These help you avoid scratches from barbed wire.

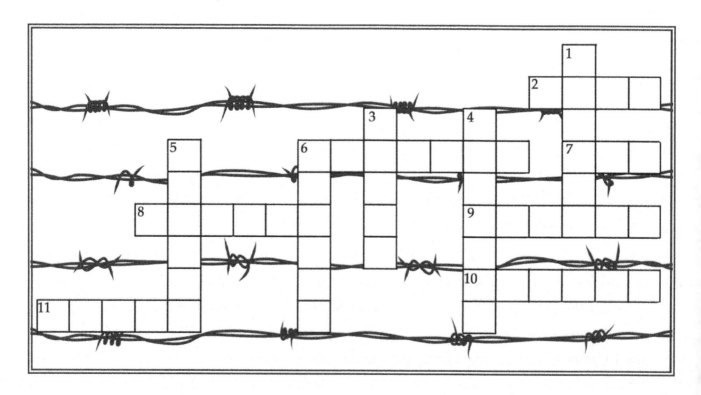

Courageous Love: Chapters 10–13

CHAPTERS 10–11

1. Who all left before dawn to catch the train back to Bay Area? _____ _____

   _____ _____ _____ _____

2. Andi wants to let Riley know what the Hollisters are like. What past memory does she use?

   _____

3. List word pictures that tell you how the Hollisters live (p. 74). Example: *crumbling outbuildings*

   _____

   _____

   _____

   _____

4. What does the Spanish word *"fuego"* mean? _____

5. Circle one: (Chad, Mother, Justin, Riley) rescues Andi from the burning barn.

6. Who does Andi believe is responsible for setting the barn on fire? _____

7. True or False: The barn burned to the ground, but they were able to save the horse tack.

CHAPTERS 12–13

8. Instead of ranch work, what does Andi find herself doing? _____

9. Why is she doing it? _____

10. True or False: Mitch comes home to help Chad restore order to the Circle C.

11. Which Circle C horse suffers the most injuries from the fire? _____

12. From which prison has the outlaw Tomaso Rodendo escaped? _____

13. Why are Mother and Chad upset when they hear Tomaso Rodendo's nickname "Procopio the Red-handed"? _____

   _____

14. What is the name of the other escaped prisoner, the one Sadie mentioned? _____

15. Justin comes out to the ranch for two reasons. One is to tell his family about Procopio's escape. What is the other reason? _____

16. What happy news does Justin share with Andi? _____

COURAGEOUS LOVE: VOCABULARY-LEARNING MEANING FROM CONTEXT

For each underlined word below, circle the closest definition for its meaning. Then use the word in a sentence of your own. (See example.)

1. Riley possessed more <u>gumption</u> than these two tired-looking cowhands combined.

   foolishness   knowledge   horses   (resourcefulness)

   It takes a lot of gumption to not give up when things go bad.

2. It was just one of the <u>hazards</u> of being the boss's sister.

   weaknesses   dangers   blessings   protections

   _____

3. He rode off, not bothering to see if the men closed the <u>makeshift</u> gate.

   thrown-together   unfinished   barbed-wire   permanent

   _____

4. "For a wrangler not yet twenty years old, you sure are acting <u>uppity</u>," Brett said.

   humble   knowledgeable   high-and-mighty   foolish

   _____

5. Sheep chewed down the grass, making it hard for the cattle to find good <u>forage</u>.

   paths   water   shelter   feed

   _____

6. "Sure, we <u>filched</u> a steer or two time and again when we was hungry," Vince said.

   killed   returned   stole   fenced

   _____

7. She didn't stop to think if it was wise to plunge headlong into the <u>inferno</u>.

   fire   danger   disturbance   hostility

   _____

8. Any <u>vigorous</u> activity took Andi's breath away.

   serious   feeble   daring   energetic

   _____

9. "A <u>skittish</u> horse shows me there's no serious nerve damage," Jake assured Chad.

   quiet   jumpy   hurting   playful

   _____

COURAGEOUS LOVE: CHARACTER CLUES

Identify these characters from *Courageous Love* by reading the following clues.

1. I knew Andi when me and her were little. My family lives up in the hills, and we can't never seem to get ahead. I don't see much of Andi anymore, but I did spy a suspicious fellow the other day and told her about him. _____

2. I offered the toast at Chad and Ellianna's engagement party.

   _____

3. I was scared to death when my aunt shoved me under a big couch. It was dark and noisy. I screamed and cried, but it didn't do any good. _____

4. I have three children, live in San Francisco, and visit the Circle C, from time to time. _____

5. I have been encouraged to become a teacher too many times to count, but I'm not interested. I have the Circle C boss's word that I can help run the ranch. _____

6. I had an accident on my horse and have been laid up with an injured back. _____

7. I saw the barn on fire, rang the bell, and cried *"fuego!"* _____

8. I did my best to rescue the Circle C horses from the burning barn. I also rescued a very foolish young lady who ran in after her colt. _____

9. I escaped from San Quentin prison and am out for revenge against the bothersome Carter family. _____

10. Those sixty Angus heifers are my pride and joy. I would be devastated if anything happened to them. _____

FAVORITE CHARACTER

Who is your favorite character so far in *Courageous Love*?

_____

Write a short paragraph describing why you chose him or her as your favorite character.

_____

_____

_____

_____

_____

Justin does his research on the criminals he has helped put behind bars. He discovers that a few of them have escaped. Chad agrees that the West is full of "leaky prisons." What were jails and prisons like in the Old West? Some were good, some were bad, and some were just plain odd. Lawbreakers, regardless of age or the severity of their crimes, were arrested and put into prison with true, murderous convicts. Here is a sampling of some Old West prisons.

ARIZONA: It took the mining town of Wickenburg, Arizona, almost thirty years to build a jail for their town. From 1863 until 1890 they chained lawbreakers to a mesquite tree in the center of town called "The Jail Tree." There the outlaws waited under the hot desert sun until the Phoenix sheriff could come get them. No one ever escaped, but apparently the tree got so crowded one time that they chained an outlaw to a log. Tired of waiting around, he picked up the log and walked over to the saloon.

TEXAS: In the nineteenth century there was no such thing as making life pleasant for outlaws. Most prisoners were treated like animals. The worst of the prisons could be found in Texas. There men were chained up in iron collars. A fourteen-year-old boy wore handcuffs that cut into his wrists. Why was this boy in a Texas prison? He had simply been in the wrong place at the wrong time—the same place where a man had been killed. In many prisons there were a number of inmates who were not guilty. Many more had mental illnesses, which (as you can guess) got worse after spending time in an Old West prison. Is it any wonder that imprisoned outlaws claimed their innocence? Some really were innocent.

NEW MEXICO: In Lincoln, New Mexico, the outlaw Billy the Kid and his pals were kept in a pit jail—a hole in the ground with a trapdoor beneath the jailer's house. Billy the Kid, however, escaped during one of his prison terms, only to be shot and killed four months later.

MONTANA: In 1874, the citizens of Helena, Montana, built a tall, elaborate, red-brick structure. It held six cells, an exercise hall, a kitchen, and a bunkhouse for the guards. However, there were no modern conveniences like electricity. It was a dismal place in spite of the fancy buildings.

IDAHO: The Idaho Territorial Prison in 1870 included a work program. Inmates labored on a fifty-acre farm just outside the prison walls. They grew most of the food for the institution.

CALIFORNIA: The first prison in California opened in 1851 aboard a ship anchored in San Francisco Bay, the *Waban*. It was outfitted to hold thirty criminals. The next year San Quentin (from where Procopio and his cohorts escape) opened near San Francisco and could hold sixty-eight prisoners. It is the oldest prison in California, is still in operation today, and can hold over 4,000 inmates. It is one of the largest prisons in the United States and even has its own zip code for mail.

COURAGEOUS LOVE: WHERE IN THE WEST?

On the map of the United States below, color the six states with prisons highlighted on the previous page. Use this code: Arizona-yellow; New Mexico-blue; California-red; Montana-orange; Idaho-green; Texas-purple.

TEST YOURSELF: How many states can you identify from memory? Use the postal zip code abbreviation to label as many as you can. (Several have been done for you as examples.)

How many states could you identify from memory? _____

Use an atlas or the Internet to find a map of the United States. Label the rest of the states. (Alaska and Hawaii are not shown on this map.) Use the Internet to find the postal abbreviations.

SOMETHING EXTRA Use the Internet to fill out the fact sheet about a prison in your state.

https://en.wikipedia.org/wiki/List_of_United_States_state_prisons

STATE	PRISON NAME	LOCATION (CITY)	YEAR IT OPENED	# OF PRISONERS	MALE OR FEMALE

Courageous Love: Chapters 14–17

CHAPTERS 14–15

1. Why does Andi pray, "Please don't let Melinda or Ellie stop by this evening for a visit"?

_____

2. What is hanging around Andi's neck that Sammy tries to grab? _____

3. Write the simile that describes Riley's face when he shows up at Andi's doorstep.

_____

4. List one clue (pages 102-103) that shows the reader Andi is embarrassed that Riley shows up.

_____

5. List one clue from pages 102-103 that shows the reader Riley is happy to see Andi.

_____

6. Write the simile from page 110 that describes how scared and upset Andi is.

_____

7. What event panics Andi so she insists on taking Lucy and the baby out to the ranch?

_____

8. List Riley's two plans for helping Andi, Lucy, and Sammy. Circle the plan they decide on.

    A. _____

    B. _____

CHAPTERS 16–17

9. Contrast the appearance of the two outlaws who burst in on Andi and Lucy.

Outlaw's Name:	Outlaw's Name:

10. Who is the shadow from Andi's past that has returned? _____

11. What surprise does Andi find in the satchel? _____

12. How does Justin describe Procopio? _____

13. What event dashes Andi's hope of making the rest of the journey bearable?

_____

COURAGEOUS LOVE: VOCABULARY—LEARNING MEANINGS FROM CONTEXT

For each of the underlined words below, write a definition in your own words. Use a dictionary for help if needed. (See example.)

1. Andi jostled Sammy in another round of horsey ride.

    "jostled" means . . . _____bounced up and down_____

2. At times, Sid, the ranch foreman, infuriated Andi with his meddling.

    "infuriated" means . . . _____

3. "He was kinda old, like my pa, but slicked up in fancy duds," the little boy said.

    "duds" are . . . _____

4. Riley's calm composure in the midst of uncertainty gave Andi a needed boost.

    "composure" is . . . _____

5. Lucy's face showed her queasiness.

    "queasiness" means . . . _____

6. Lucy hurried from the room with a satchel in her hand.

    a "satchel" is . . . _____

7. Andi squirmed to free herself, but her unknown assailant tightened his grip.

    "assailant" means . . . _____

8. The bandit's cohort, however, didn't appear to care about his own appearance.

    a "cohort" is . . . _____

9. Andi nodded her compliance and reached for Sammy.

    "compliance" means . . . _____

10. If riled, Tucker could take a good chunk out of the ruffian's leg.

    a "ruffian" is . . . _____

11. Andi felt wrapped up tighter than a lunatic in an asylum.

    "a lunatic" is . . . _____

12. Seeing the buggy go into the river sent Andi's heart plummeting to her belly.

    "plummeting" means . . . _____

13. Lucy had hidden a derringer in the satchel.

    a "derringer" is . . . _____

At the end of chapter 16, Tomaso Procopio Rodendo writes a note and signs his name with a flourish before nailing the paper to Justin's screen door frame. He has revenge in mind, and he feels justified. Where does the expression "an eye for an eye" come from, and what does it mean?

"An eye for an eye" is the law of retaliation or vengeance. It's the right of injured persons to pay back those who injured them in the same way they were injured (or had a crime committed against them). It goes back to ancient times. For example, in 1754 BC, the Code of Hammurabi included "an eye for an eye and a tooth for a tooth" as part of its law.

The Old Testament also mentions retaliation in many places. "If a man injures his neighbor, just as he has done, so it shall be done to him: fracture for fracture, eye for eye, tooth for tooth; just as he has injured a man, so it shall be inflicted on him." (Lev. 24:19–20 NASB). It's important to realize that the punishment could not go *beyond* what had been done to the victim. This kept the victim from taking the law into his own hands and exacting more payback than was allowed. It's also important to realize that the offender usually paid back the injured person with money to compensate for his loss (instead of blinding him or knocking out his tooth). If not, most of the nation of Israel would have ended up blind and toothless.

When Jesus walked this earth, he knew the law well. He went beyond the principle of seeking vengeance (payback) and preached forgiveness. Find Matthew 5:38-39 and copy the verses:

1. _____

_____

_____

2. Another important verse is Romans 12:19. Write it here: _____

_____

_____

3. Christ fulfilled the Law. Christians do not follow the old "eye for an eye and tooth for a tooth" principle. We are free to follow a higher law. Find Galatians 6:2 and write the name of this law.

_____

4. Read Colossians 3:13. In your own words write what this law means.

_____

POP QUIZ: Procopio the Red-handed wrote the message to Justin in English. How did he say this phrase in Spanish? (See page 115 in *Courageous Love*.) _____

Courageous Love: Spanish

Most of the Circle C Milestones books contain plenty of Spanish. Nineteenth-century California was populated by a good number of Mexicans and *Californios* (Spanish-speaking persons of Latin American descent born in California). It was to the ranchers' benefit to be fluent in both English and Spanish, which the Carter family is. Andi's very life—and the lives of her sister-in-law and baby nephew—depends on her knowing what their captors plan to do. She is wise to not let them figure out that she can understand them.

Can you understand the Spanish in this story? Chapters 16 and 17 are full of Spanish words and phrases. Every one of them can be figured out by context (reading the words before or after the character uses the Spanish words). You do not need a Spanish-English dictionary or the Internet. How to pronounce the words is also given. Impress your family and friends with your knowledge of the language!

The accent marks show where to put the stress on the sound. For example, in English you pronounce "popcorn" as *pópcorn*, with an accent mark over the "o" to show which part of the word stress. You pronounce "unique" as *u-neék*, with the accent on the second syllable.

Match the Spanish words with their English translations from the word box below. Then pronounce each word aloud. (Pages numbers are given for context.)

1. _____ Jefe (*héy-fey*) p. 113

2. _____ ¡Qué gatita montésa! (*kay gah-tí-ta mohn-táy-sa*) p. 114

3. _____ ¡Basta ya! (*báhs-ta ya*) p. 114

4. _____ Ojo por ojo (*óh-ho poor óh-ho*) p. 115

5. _____ Mis compadres (*mees cohm-pá-dres*) p. 115

6. _____ Bueno. Vámonos. (*bwáy-no. Báh-moh-nohs*) p. 116

7. _____ Chica (*cheé-kah*) p. 116

8. _____ ¿Comprende? (*cohm-prén-day*) p. 116

9. _____ Por favor (*poor fah-vór*) p. 116

10. _____ ¡Más rápido! (*mahs rá-pee-doh*) p. 122

A. Good. Let's go.

B. Boss

C. Faster!

D. girl

E. What a little wildcat!

F. Do you understand?

G. My companions

H. That's enough!

I. Please

J. Eye for an eye

Courageous Love: Chapters 18–21

Show how well you understand the story by answering the following questions.

CHAPTERS 18–19

1. Procopio orders his men around in Spanish. Which Spanish word means "hurry up"?

_____Which Spanish word means "Let's go"? _____

2. Who quietly warns Andi not to antagonize Procopio? _____

3. To visualize the small company as they travel, list who is riding with whom. Procopio: _____ Jed: _____ Vega: _____

4.   Why does Procopio call his first rest stop? _____

_____

5. Find the simile from the top of page 132 that describes Jed's never-ending chatter: _____

6. What is Andi sure of after hearing Jed talk about his stay in San Quentin?

   A. He has paid his debt for his crime and is now as free as any man.

   B. His mind has become twisted during his prison time.

   C. He is a changed man and sorry for all the trouble he caused Andi five years ago.

7.   Where is Procopio's robber band is located? _____

CHAPTERS 20–21

8. During their second rest of the night, Vega and Procopio leave camp. Why? _____

_____

9. Andi learns the reason the two outlaws did not set fire to the rancher's home is because *"nos faltó tiempo."* What does this mean (p. 140)? _____

10. The girls are finally allowed to ride separately. Why does Andi offer to ride Thunder?

_____

11. How many nights and days do they spend on the journey to Procopio's hideout? (Hint: Their journey began in the evening, so count the nights first.)   **Nights**: _____ **Days:** _____

12. To their horror, Andi and Lucy learn the real meaning of Procopio's *ojo por ojo*. What is the bandit's vengeance? _____

13. What is Sammy's new name? _____

14. Andi's first chore at the outlaws' camp is _____

15. What surprise greets Andi in the woods? _____

COURAGEOUS LOVE: VOCABULARY CIRCLE PUZZLE

Use the clues to fill out each vocabulary word. Then use the letters in the circles to find out who Andi hopes will come to their rescue. (The first one has been done, and page numbers are given.)

1. Andi's thoughts swirled in [disorder, confusion, an uproar]. (page 127)

(T) U R M O I L

2. Every one of these people were [delighted, overjoyed] at Procopio's return. (page 144)

___ Ⓞ ___ ___ ___ ___ ___ ___

3. "You are strong and quick—and quite [attractive; nice to look at]." (page 148)

Ⓞ ___ ___ ___ ___ ___

4. "He's got a hideout near the north fork of the [the name of a river] River." (page 134)

Ⓞ ___ ___ ___ ___

5. Jed was warning Andi not to [provoke, irritate, annoy] the Mexican outlaw. (page 125)

___ ___ ___ ___ ___ ___ ___ ___ Ⓞ

6. Andi would remember that God had the last say in this [trial, trouble]. (page 128)

___ Ⓞ ___ ___ ___ ___

7. Andi rode in a daze, exhausted, filthy, and [depressed, unhappy]. (page 142)

___ ___ ___ ___ Ⓞ ___ ___

8. Twilight had given way to a deep, [dark blue] sky. (page 125)

___ Ⓞ ___ ___ ___ ___

9. Andi met Jed's sympathy with a [bold, rebellious] sneer. (page 147)

Ⓞ ___ ___ ___ ___ ___ ___

10. Procopio's parting note had said nothing about any [payment, exchange]. (page 134)

Ⓞ ___ ___ ___ ___ ___

11. The Mexican outlaw was [cunning, shrewd] and knew how to outsmart trackers. (page 128)

___ Ⓞ ___ ___

12. Jed's mount seemed to [stumble, trip] over every submerged rock. (page 128)

___ ___ Ⓞ ___ ___ ___

13. Jed . . . [tied] the other end around the saddle horn of his buckskin horse. (page 125)

___ ___ ___ ___ ___ Ⓞ ___

14. "If it pleases Jed to [busy, interest] his head with dreams of gold, I will allow it." (page 148)

___ ___ ___ ___ ___ ___ Ⓞ ___ ___

T ___

Procopio (also known as Red-handed Dick and Red Dick) was one of the best-known bandits in Californian history. He got his nickname either from his red hair (unlikely) or because of his violent nature and bloodthirstiness. In 1872, the *San Francisco Chronicle* called him "one of the most fearless and daring desperadoes . . . of our state." Some newspapers compared him to Robin Hood. Procopio was often aided in escaping from lawmen by Mexicans living in California.

Tomaso was born in Mexico around 1841. His father was a *vaquero* (cowboy), and his mother was the oldest sister of the most notorious bandit in California history—Joaquin Murrieta. Young Tomaso and his parents came to the United States in 1853, the same year rangers killed Tomaso's uncle. The rangers kept Murrieta's head in a jar of brandy and displayed it around California for $1 a peek. It is said that Procopio witnessed his uncle's death, idolized his uncle, and later grew into a fearless rider and a reckless youth.

Procopio's first involvement with crime occurred in 1862 when he was suspected of the murder of a southern California rancher. But there was not enough evidence to charge him with the crime. He fled north after that and soon became the leader of a bandit gang that engaged in nighttime raids on farms and ranches in the area. In 1863, the gang was suspected in the brutal murder of a rancher, his wife, and his two children. The house was burned to the ground. Procopio was freed again for lack of evidence.

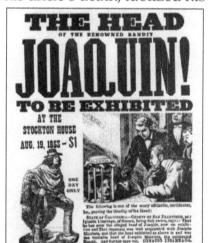

He was finally caught stealing *a lot* of cattle from a rancher named Pope. Procopio took full blame, served nine years in San Quentin, and was released in 1871. Did he learn his lesson? Not according to the *Alameda Gazette*: Procopio "returned to his old practices as a dog to vomit." He teamed up with the bandit Tiburcio Vasquez and robbed the Visalia stagecoach. The passengers aboard the coach, four men and a woman, were tied up and robbed of two gold watches and $500 in gold. An 1871 newspaper noted that Procopio and his gang were "splendidly mounted and equipped, wear good clothes and sport gold watches."

Following a few more stagecoach robberies, Procopio and Vasquez headed to Mexico to spend their new wealth. When they returned, Vasquez headed for the hills but Procopio stayed in San Francisco, where he was caught and arrested. The case drew attention all the way back east. *The New York Times* reported: "Tomas Rodundo, alias Procopio, who is charged with many murders and stage robberies, and other crimes, was captured today at his hiding place in San Francisco.

He has been the terror of Southern California for years. He was surprised today, and had not time to draw his pistols, or, it is said, he would never have been taken alive."

But, as usual, the law could not find sufficient evidence to convict him of the murders. Instead of a life sentence for murder, Procopio was back at San Quentin for another seven years.

Procopio was out again in 1877 and returned to banditry, leading a gang in raids near Fresno, Grangeville, and Caliente. Procopio and his gang were captured near the Tejon Pass, and five members of his gang were lynched in Bakersfield in 1878. However, Procopio escaped, formed a new gang, and went back to his robbing ways. A slippery bandit indeed!

No one is sure what happened to the bandit after that. Some say he kept robbing. Others say he was arrested in Arizona in 1883. One account reports that Procopio shot and killed an actor in Mexico, was arrested, and was executed by a firing squad. Another account states that he returned to Mexico and served in the army. Some stories suggest that he died in the early 1890s. Who really knows? His life became a legend blown out of proportion. Men would pale when they heard his name, and mothers would use Procopio the Red-handed to scare their children into behaving.

WHO AM I?

1. Tomaso idolized me. He was a great kid, and I wish I could have seen him grow up. However, some California rangers tracked me down, killed me, and stuffed my head in a jar. Such disrespect! Worse, they showed me off at exhibitions all over the state. Who am I? _____

2. It was a great idea to team up with Procopio the Red-handed. I met him when he got out of prison, and we went right to work robbing so many stagecoaches that I lost track. We always dressed sharp too. Who am I? _____

3. I was a cowboy (*vaquero*) by trade. I took my family to the United States, but it might have been better for my son if we had stayed in Mexico. Who am I? _____

4. I will never be able to live up to my Uncle Joaquin's fame in California, but I tried. I led a gang of bandits, and we terrorized the farms and ranches wherever we went. I went to prison twice, but never for murder. They couldn't find enough evidence to convict me. But I'll tell you right now . . . I did kill those ranchers. Who am I? _____

5. Thanks to me, the outlaw Procopio finally got caught. He stole a lot of my cattle, but luckily the law tracked him down. I was one of the lucky ones. He didn't kill me. Who am I?

_____

Courageous Love: Chapters 22–26

CHAPTERS 22–24

1. How long have Andi, Lucy, and Sammy been at the camp? _____

2. What verse does Andi repeat to herself when she is especially worried? _____
_____

3. What secret does Lucy share with Andi? _____
_____

4. What is the name of the beaten and weary traveler who shows up at the bandits' hideout?
_____ What is his real name? _____

5. How does this man get Procopio to accept him? _____

6. Ramón's uncle in this story was Procopio's real-life compadre. What is his name?
_____ True or false? He may show up show up at camp at any moment.

7. To whom does Andi reveal that she speaks Spanish as well as any of the Mexican bandits?

      A. Procopio   B. Benita   C. Vega   D. Jed

8. Who surprises Andi by saving her life? _____

9. How do Lucy and Sammy escape? _____

CHAPTERS 25–26

10. Andi's journal entry states *"God forgive me. I did what I had to do . . ."* What has Andi
done that she needs to ask forgiveness? _____

11. Andi is shocked when Riley gallops toward her on Dakota because . . .

    A. He is alive.   B. He's wounded and bleeding.   C. He intends to use the pickup trick.

12. What is Andi's reaction to the overwhelming relief that she is safe and that Procopio and his
band have most likely been caught? _____

13. List what happens to each of these characters, then circle the character (or characters) you
know from reading the chapters are dead:

    Vega: _____   Benita: _____

    Procopio: _____   Jed: _____

14. What is Andi's wedding date? _____

15. Which family member does not attend the wedding? _____

16. Why isn't this family member in attendance? _____

17. What is the name of Justin and Lucy's new baby? _____

I am nearing the end of my rope. If I let go, I'll drop into a pit of despair, much like where Christian found himself in Pilgrim's Progress. —Andi's Journal Chapter 22

Andi likens her ordeal to that of a character from the book *The Pilgrim's Progress*:

"Just as [Christian and Pliable] had ended this talk, they drew near to a very miry slough [swamp] that was in the midst of the plain; and they being heedless, did both fall suddenly into the bog. The name of the slough was 'Despond' [Despair]. Here, therefore, they wallowed for a time, being grievously bedaubed with the dirt; and Christian, because of the burden that was on his back, began to sink in the mire."

If you would like to see how Christian and Pliable escape this horrible place, carefully copy this web address into your Internet browser.

www.covenantofgrace.com/pilgrims_progress_slough_of_despond.htm

The Pilgrim's Progress is a free, public-domain book and well worth your time to read. John Bunyan wrote this famous book—which went on to become one of the most published books in the English language—while serving prison time for his crime: preaching the gospel without permission from the Church of England. John was arrested and warned, but he refused to back down, earning him twelve long years in jail. He was released in 1672. Six years later his book was published.

The Pilgrim's Progress is an allegory (a story with a hidden meaning used to teach a lesson) about our spiritual journey from this sinful world (The City of Destruction) to heaven (The Celestial City).

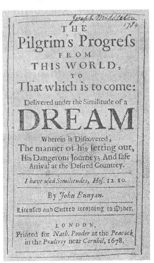

The main character, Christian, carries a burden (his knowledge of sin comes from reading The Book) from which he seeks deliverance. He leaves everything to find it. Christian has a number of adventures along the way, like falling into the slough, being trapped in a giant's Doubting Castle, and traveling alone through the terrifying Valley of the Shadow of Death. He meets friends along the way (as well as enemies who try to hinder his journey) and eventually arrives in The Celestial City.

John Bunyan was gifted with the ability to take spiritual truths from the Bible and write about them in a way ordinary people from all walks of life could understand. Besides the Bible, *The Pilgrim's Progress* is one of the best-loved and most-read books of all time.

The three-night and three-day journey to Procopio's hideout is a grueling trip for Andi, Lucy, and Samuel. Below is a map of the area through which they travel. Follow the instructions below to mark the journey and the landmarks on the map.

1. The bandits kidnap Andi, Lucy, and Sammy from Justin's home in Fresno. Fresno is the black dot in the middle of the valley. Label **Fresno**.

2. Label the **San Joaquin River** (north of Fresno).

3. Find the black starburst and label it **Bandits' Camp**.

4. The camp is close to but not actually along the North Fork of the King's River. Label the river **North Fork**.

5. The North Fork flows southwest into the main **King's River**. Label this river.

6. Label the small black dot on the King's River **Centerville**.

7. With a red pencil, start in Fresno and draw Andi's journey from Fresno to the river. Follow the San Joaquin until the river begins to twist and turn (this means it is flowing through the hills). Draw a line cross-country, but make sure it is not a straight line! They have to go around many hills and valleys. Cross Dinkey Creek and end Andi's journey at the bandits' camp.

8. In chapter 23, Ramón (Riley in disguise) presents sacks of money from the Bank of Centerville. Using a green pencil, trace Riley's route (and the route of the posse) from Centerville to the small triangle just outside the camp. This is where Lucy ends up, as well as the place where Riley eventually takes Andi.

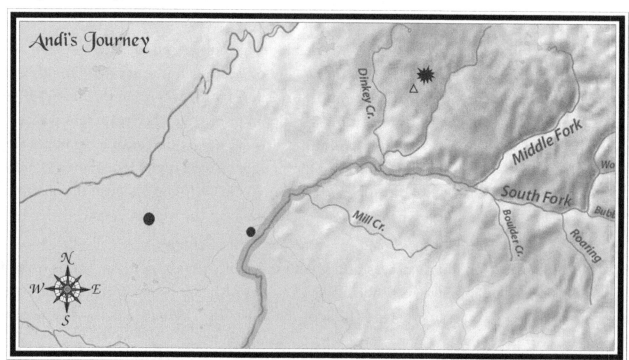

COURAGEOUS LOVE: POINT OF VIEW

A story's point of view is simply whoever is telling the story. The character telling the story in *Courageous Love* is Andi. She is the point-of-view character. The story unfolds through her senses (eyes, ears, etc.) and her thoughts. Since Andi can't know anything she can't see or hear, the reader cannot know it either. This is the reason the reader doesn't know what has happened to Riley the night they are kidnapped.

It's fun to imagine what a scene or chapter might look like if the story was unfolding from another character's point of view. For instance, what if we could see the scene from Tucker's point of view back in chapter 16? On page 117, Tucker is lying under the porch swing. This is how the scene would read from the dog's point of view.

> Tucker lay poised, waiting for a signal. Ears pricked, he followed Andi's every movement. He wanted nothing more than to take a big chunk out of those strange men's legs. *Come on, Andi! Give me the signal. I can chew them up!*
>
> To his dismay, Andi *did* give him a signal. The wrong signal. The "stay" signal. No matter how much Tucker wanted to disobey and go after those men, he did not. He laid his head on his paws and watched Andi, Lucy, and Sammy walk toward a buggy. As soon as they left, Tucker would find his master. Then he would go after Andi.

It's fun to imagine how other characters would make their way through a story scene. What about Riley? How does he find help later on? How does he get hold of the bank gold? What is Lucy feeling during her stay in the bandits' camp? How does little Samuel adjust to being snatched from his mother? It might be interesting to think about what is going through Jed Hatton's mind or even through Procopio the Red-handed's head. How does Justin react when he learns his wife, his child, and his sister are gone? What does he think when he finds the "eye for an eye" note?

YOUR TURN

Choose one of the characters from *Courageous Love* and write (in your own words) any of the scenes from chapters 17 through the end of the book. You can also create a scene only mentioned in the book, like Justin in San Francisco or Riley's part in planning the rescue. Write the scene from the character's point of view (not Andi's). You may create your scene on the computer, print it out, and tape it to the next page. Or you may use the next page to create your scene with pencil or pen. Use description, dialogue, and thoughts. Have fun! A few characters are listed below, but you don't need to limit yourself to these.

SAMUEL JAMES	LUCY CARTER	RILEY PRESCOTT
VEGA	JED HATTON	JUSTIN CARTER
TUCKER	BENITA	PROCOPIO

SCENE WRITTEN FROM ______________________________ POINT OF VIEW

Page 9: Chapters 1-4

Chapters 1-2:

1. California; San Joaquin Valley; winter, 1882
2. She wants them to check on Taffy
3. Justin
4. a dime novel
5. B
6. overalls

Chapters 3-4:

7. There are two foals.
8. Shasta: chocolate palomino (dark body; flaxen mane);
   Sunny: cream-colored all over
9. go inside to bed
10. stay out in the barn with Taffy and the foals
11. A commission is a percentage of the money Andi would get for showing the foals.
12. whorls
13. She has to go back to school.

Page 10: Chapters 1-4

Vocabulary

1. B   noun
2. A   noun
3. C   verb
4. A   adjective
5. B   adjective
6. D   verb
7. A   adjective
8. C   adjective
9. D   verb
10. B   noun

Pages 11: Characterization

1. Andi is jumpy when Taffy is pacing and pawing; she dashes up the stairs; runs into the house for help
2. She tosses aside a thick, dark braid.
3. dark; long; braid
4. Andi wants Chad "right now!"; she tells Justin to "hurry"
5. Answers may include:
   - Chad's the best stockman in the valley.
   - He yells when he's annoyed or upset.
   - He and Andi are a lot alike.
   - Chad is impulsive and quick-tempered.
   - He is calm in an emergency.
   - He is protective and knows how to make Andi feel better.

Page 13: Foal Crossword Puzzle

Across	Down:
5. stallion	1. teat
6. runt	2. thirty
7. ninety	3. eleven
11. ultrasound	4. unpredictable
	8. mare
	9. udder
	10. foal

Page 15:

Synonyms & Antonyms

Chapters 5-8

1. clear   opaque
2. distant   friendly
3. shocking   dull
4. understanding   unfeeling
5. stuffy   airy
6. fearful   brave
7. flighty   predictable
8. awful   wonderful
9. captivated   distracted
10. weakly   brightly

Page 14: Chapters 5-8

Chapters 5-6

1. February
2. Sixteen
3. Grammar
4. Andi's time with the colts is cut way back.
5. Subject = building; verb = is
6. winks at her
7. Marcella Walker

Chapters 7-8

8. B
9. Virginia
10. The colts are being weaned.
11. A
12. Four years ago
13. Lucinda (Lucy) Hawkins
14. Melinda

Answer Key: *Thick as Thieves* - 2

Page 16: School Math

1. <u>2</u> ft x <u>10</u> ft. x <u>3</u> ft. = <u>60</u> cubic feet; <u>60</u> divided by <u>1.2</u> = **50 bushels of wheat**

2. <u>2,000</u> pounds = 1 ton; <u>6,720</u> pounds divided by <u>2,000</u> = <u>3.36</u> tons; 3.36 x <u>$6.00</u> = **$20.16 for the coal.**

Page 18: Foal-training Timeline

NEWBORN: Rub the foal all over; sit in a corner and watch the foal

A FEW DAYS OLD: Teach the foal who is boss; spend all your time with the foal; teach the cold to stand still; put an arm around his chest and another arm around his rump.

ONE WEEK OLD: Put a halter on the foal for 15 minutes.

TWO WEEKS OLD: Teach the colt to stand tied; teach the colt to lead with a halter and lead rope

ONE TO TWO MONTHS: Teach the colt the word "no."

FIVE TO SIX MONTHS: Wean the foal from his dam.

ONE YEAR OLD: Start lunging the colt in a round pen; teach the colt to "walk," "stop," and "trot" on command.

TWO TO THREE YEARS: Train the colt to be ridden.

Page 21: Chapters 9-12
Chapters 9-10
1. **SHASTA**: flaxen mane; chocolate body; no stripes or socks; smart; calm **SUNNY:** smaller colt; cream-colored (like a sunbeam) mischievous; impulsive; startles easily
2. Hector Flores
3. C
4. false
5. Andi gives Macy her old McGuffey's primer to read.
6. C
Chapters 11-12
7. Macy gave Cory another black eye; stole Ollie's bat; grabbed the ball; cut up the jump rope; stole the boys' marbles; dumped water on Andi
8. Andi sees Macy picking on Cindy and snatching her doll.
9. false

Page 22: Vocabulary Matching
Chapters 9-12

1. D	7. C
2. G	8. K
3. B	9. E
4. J	10. F
5. A	11. H
6. I	

Digging Deeper: Answers will vary.

Page 23: A "Lousy" Poem
One **LOUSE**, two **LICE**. Finding them is not real **NICE**. A half-grown **NYMPH** was once a **NIT**. If your heads starts to itch, you know you've been **BIT.**

Page 24: Chapters 13-16
Chapters 13-14
1. Andi can dream and make plans all she likes, but she knows she can't get away with putting her journal plans into practice. So, the journal entry is "fiction" (her imagination) to her.
2. (any of these): Lucy can drive a buggy well; She lives in Fresno and keeps house for her lawyer-brother; Lucy is from San Francisco; Lucy's family is delighted that she's marrying Justin; Lucy has dark-brown hair; She has dimples; She can drive a buggy; She seems to like Andi.
3. Taffy tries to scrape Andi off.
4. Answers will vary, but something about being angry at the things that anger God: sin and injustice, etc.
5. Andi offers Macy a ride on Taffy.
Chapters 15-16
6. Mitch doesn't bring it up. He saddles Taffy for her. He gives her quiet approval at what she chose with Macy.
7. a tack
8. He offers to carry her books.
9. Ty, Jase, and Rudy   10. Jase   11. go out to their place in the canyon (or) help Rudy keep an eye on things

Page 27: Vocabulary Chapters 13-16 (sample answers)

1. To skip out; not go
2. To delay or waver
3. It's certain.
4. A real or genuine reason
5. Embarrassed or humiliated
6. A blood-sucking worm
7. The most visited saloons
8. Sin
9. To push or prod
10. To baby or pamper someone
11. Hanging around
12. Slang for being "hanged"

Page 28: Similes

1. She bolted—streaking down K Street [like a shot out of last summer's Fourth of July cannon.]
2. It compares Taffy's speed to a cannon shot.
3. Taffy was running fast!
4. Andi stayed in the saddle by clinging to Taffy's neck [like a leech.]
5. It compares Andi's grip to a leech.
6. Andi was holding on very tightly!
7. "They got worse manners than a weasel in a henhouse."
8. It compares the brothers' manners to a weasel.
9. Macy's brothers have horrible, sneaky manners.
10. "All flesh is like grass, and all its glory like the flower of grass. The grass withers and the flower falls off ."
11. People's lives are very short.
12. Answers will vary. Check to see the student has used a simile with "like." "as." or "than."

Page 29: Chapters 17-21

Chapters 17-19

1. She is exhausted from working so hard.
2. Macy knows her brothers are the rustlers.
3. C
4. Andi decides to care about Macy rather than reject her.
5. A

Chapters 20-21

6. Andi's colts are gone (stolen).
7. She wants Chad to get her colts back.
8. Rock Canyon
9. It's dangerous
10. B
11. Peace

Page. 30: Vocab Ch. 17-21

1. Helpless
2. Scolding
3. Begging
4. Awe-struck
5. Strangest
6. Squashed
7. Manners
8. Gigantic
9. Cautious

Page 32: Cattle Rustling

Then: horseback, "ghost" riders, changed brands, hanged rustlers.

Now: trucks and trailers, fake bills of sale, $20,000 fine; 20 years in prison

Both: large industry; thousands of cattle stolen; hard to track down and catch rustlers

Page 33: Chapters 22-26

Chapters 22-24

1. Andi does not want to disappear without an explanation. She wants her family to know where she is.
2. The canyon's cliffs are compared to sentries.
3. Guards
4. **SIGHTS**: a huge disk (moon); the dark cliffs; debris; rockslide; carcasses; scrub brush; yellow light; **SOUNDS:** clip-clop of hooves; marbles tossed down stairs; crickets; frogs; cattle lowing; falling rubble; nickers; clattering and shouting from the cabin; **SMELLS**: stink along the path; stink from swollen carcasses; rotting flesh
5. Andi rescues all of the Carters' colts, not just Shasta and Sunny.
6. A rockslide and being thrown from Taffy.
7. Macy tells her brothers Andi is worth a lot of money to her family and should be ransomed instead of killed.

Page 33: Chapters 25-26

8. Macy decides to leave her brothers and stay with Andi and her family.
9. a pistol
10. Jase (or) Chad and Mitch
11. Andi gives Sunny to Macy.

Answer Key: *Thick as Thieves* – 4

Page 34: Vocabulary Crossword

ACROSS	DOWN	
4. Cower	1. Tendril	12. Niggling
5. Reinforce	2. Roiled	13. Secluded
8. Hazardous	3. Potential	16. Settee
14. Luxurious	6. Banishing	17. Bloated
15. Skeptical	7. Dumbstruck	20. Grisly
16. Sentinel	9. Dwarfing	
18. Mingled	10. Flanked	
19. Plight	11. Hummocks	

Answer Key: *Heartbreak Trail* - 1

Page 41: Chapters 1-4
Chapters 1-2
1. 14 years old, almost 15
2. Go along on the upcoming cattle drive.
3. C
4. Sid; foreman
5. B
6. Get the "ranching" notion out of her head (that she thinks she can help run the ranch).

Chapters 3-4
7. A
8. They flip a coin.
9. A collection of horses.
10. C
11. Kitty Wilkins and Lizzie Williams
12. Justin

Page 42: Elements of a Fiction Story
1. Examples: Levi = nephew; Chad = brother; Sid = foreman over Andi; Justin = brother; Elizabeth = mother; Lucy = future sister-in-law; Melinda = sister; Mitch = brother.
2. spring 1883
3. Circle C Ranch
4. Tulare Lake; Buena Vista Lake
5. See the map on page 6 of the book for placements.

Page 44 Chapters 1-4 Vocabulary & Grammar
1. C adjective
2. A verb
3. B verb
4. D verb
5. C verb
6. A noun
7. B verb
8. D adjective
9. A verb

Page 46 Word Search

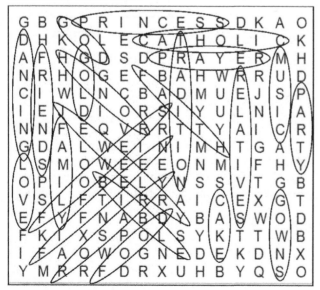

Page 47 Chapters 5-8
Chapters 5-6
1. Partially lame; a Mexican; old and proud; gruff; hard-working; bossy
2. 1,000 head of cattle
3. B
4. She hopes to get a ride on Toledo's beautiful horse.
5. Sultan; white; black
6. She thinks Mitch left without her because she slept in.

Chapters 7-8
7. Flint doesn't like horses, yet he does the job given to him without complaining.
8. Answers will vary: a seagoing dinosaur
9. Chad takes her out to see the herd bedded down.
10. **SETTING**: see the map in the book on page 6. They have traveled 4 days; They have gone 55 miles.

Page 48: Chapters 5-8
Vocabulary
1. Immediately
2. Removed
3. Commotion
4. Complained
5. Hindrance
6. Boasting
7. Delighting
8. Captivated
9. Faded

Page 49:
Spanish
1. D
2. G
3. B
4. H
5. C
6. A
7. F
8. I
9. E

Page 50: Trail Jobs

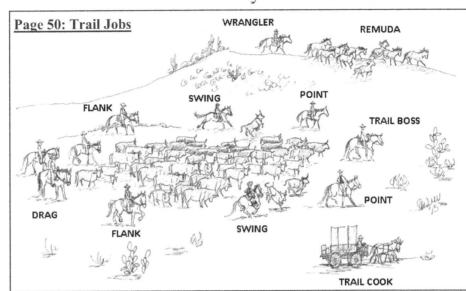

Page 53: Chapters 9-12
Chapters 9-10
1. C
2. He's the trail boss.
3. A
4. grinding coffee beans (or) making coffee.
5. frying the bacon.
6. mosquitoes
7. false

Chapters 11-12
8. the ague (marsh fever or malaria)
9. her eyes are bright & clear; no fever; it's too soon for the disease to show up.
10. ginger tea; dizziness
11. They see two men around a campfire.
12. She has dirt on her face and looks messy.
13. camels; Tejon

Page 54: Chapters 9-12 Vocabulary
1. D	7. A	**Digging Deeper:**
2. K	8. C	Answers will vary.
3. G	9. E	
4. F	10. B	
5. J	11. I	
6. H		

Page 56: Escape the Wetlands

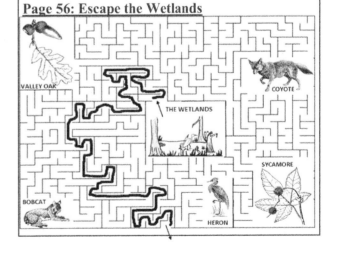

Page 57: Spanish
1. Levántate
2. Arriba
3. Ven aquí
4. Qué pasa
5. Está bien
6. Tómalo
7. No importa
8. Hombres
9. Ándale
10. Dónde está Levi
11. Comprende

Spanish Review
1. food; meal
2. Many thanks
3. Good day/morning
4. Hurry up!
5. I don't need help.
6. There is water.
7. Go away/Get going!
8. Sit down.

Answer Key: *Heartbreak Trail* - 3

Page 60: Chapters 13-16
Chapters 13-14
1. Andi decides to stick out the drive and not give up.
2. See map on page 6 of the book. "X" should be placed where the trail crosses the Kern River.
3. B
4. Because the river is too high, and the current is fast.
5. Cook jumps off to help the horses reach the other side.
6. Mitch narrowly escapes being gored; the cattle stampede; the horses stir up the cattle
Chapters 15-16
7. Cattails should be placed to the south of Bakersfield.
8. Andi took off on Sultan with Toledo's say-so.
9. Because Toledo is unpredictable. No one knows when he will explode, or when he will act and speak nicely.
10. Chad; Huey; Bryce
11. Andi decides she wants to go home as soon as she can.
12. 3 gunshots

Page 61:
Chapters 13-16
Vocabulary
1. alarming
2. tilted
3. thrashing
4. exhaustion
5. wild
6. recover
7. unfaltering
8. supplied
9. coming together

Page 62: Spanish part 3
1. I don't like it.
2. Silence (or be quiet), girl.
3. Yes, sir.
4. Don't worry.
5. Thank God!
6. Enough!
Digger Deeper
1. She is determined; competitive: sample traits: stubborn, hardy, energetic, bold, not lazy.
2.-4. Answers will vary.

Page 68: Chapters 17-20
Chapters 17-18
1. See map on page 6 of the book.
2. Andi remembers the time when her brother Mitch was shot.
3. fast
4. They are the same men she and Levi saw in the woods.
5. Huey: he's gone; Chad: he's shot; Bryce: he's dead; Wyatt: sprained wrist
6. wrangler
Chapters 19-20
7. Andi: wrangler; Flint: drag rider; Levi: drag rider; Rico: Cook's helper
8. Dusty is an excellent "boss" horse, making Andi's job easy.
9. false
10. Cook
11. Toledo
12. Toledo is a thief and a scoundrel; he steals cattle.

Page 69: Chapters 17-20 Vocabulary
1. ambushed; attacked
2. faint; pass out
3. leap; fly from
4. laugh
5. smug; overconfident
6. unplanned
7. magnitude; huge size
8. disaster; tragedy
9. lifted
10. sneaky; devious
11. worn out; exhausted
12. confused; puzzled
13. unaffected

Page 70 Map Work
1. San Joaquin Valley
2. Grapevine Canyon
3. Tehachapi Mts.
4. Mojave Desert

Page 71 Fort Tejon Riddles
1. Barracks
2. Grapevine Canyon
3. Camels
4. Dragoons (or) soldiers
5. Civilians (local residents)

Page 72: Chapters 21-25
Chapters 21-23
1. Santa Monica Mts. are to the north of LA. The pass is in the middle of the mountains. Los Angeles is the dot.
2. C
3. No. Toledo whistles; his horse comes running.
4. "Get out the six-shooters." "Let's chase after him." "We need our beef back." "We should round up some men."
5. **CC hands**: Wyatt, Diego, Flint, Cook, Joselito
   Temporary: Toledo, Huey, Kirby, Tripp, Seth, Bryce
6. Toledo shows up with his band of thieves and kidnaps Andi and Levi.
Chapters 24-25
7. a livery stable
8. A
9. have a party with music, dancing, and a pretty dress.
10. B

Page 73: Spanish Part 4
1. I
2. J
3. E
4. A
5. C
6. H
7. D
8. G
9. F
10. B

Page 73: Story Problem and Plot Events
1. Andi wants to go on the cattle drive. Once on the drive, she must overcome the problem that she has "bitten off more than she can chew."
2. A. down; B. up; C. down; D. up; E. up; F. down; G. down; H. up; I. up; J. down; K. up; L. down; M. up

Page 74: Los Angeles
1. Butterfly
2. The Tar
3. The Cats
4. Sacrament
5. Holy Cross
6. Saint John the Baptist
7. Riverview
8. Holy Faith
9. The Crosses
10. Mountain of the King
11. Saint Matthew
12. Blood of Christ

Page 79: Chapters 1–5
Chapters 1–3
1. New York City; Aunt Lydia Carter
2. G, D, F, E, I, H, A C, B
3. Chad has hired a young wrangler to work with the colts.
4. Riley Prescott
5. ten years; the funeral for Andi's father, James.
6. Any of these: pinched Melinda; put snakes in Melinda's bed; swiped eggs from the henhouse; nearly drowned the cat; bullied the girls; let the horses loose from their stalls
Ch. 4–5
7. Mitch
8. not protecting her skin; her nickname, Andi.
9. Horses
10. thrown from his horse in a roundup accident
11. a square dance.

Page 81: God's Word

GREEK MYTH	SCRIPTURE
Pandora	Eve
from clay	from Adam's rib
Don't open the box.	Don't eat from the tree.
Zeus	God
She opened the box.	She ate from the tree.
Sin entered the world.	Sin entered the world.
no hope	Jesus Christ

Page 82: Ch. 1-5
Vocabulary & Grammar
1. C verb
2. A adjective
3. B adjective
4. D noun
5. B adjective
6. A adjective
7. C adjective
8. B verb
9. A noun

Answer Key: *The Last Ride* – 2

Page 84: The Route

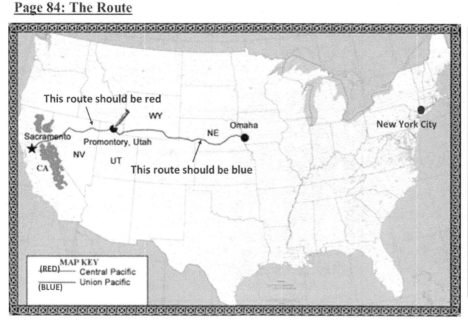

Page 85: The Math

1. Union Pacific RR won the race by **397** miles (1,087 – 690 = 397).
2. Total length of track laid: **1,777** (1,087 + 690 = 1,777)
3. It would take about **35 ½ years**. (1,777 divided by 50 miles a year = 35.54).
4. **6 years**. (1869–1863)
5. They could lay **70 miles** in 7 days (10 miles a day x 7 days = 70 miles of track).

Page 86: Chapters 6–9
Chapters 6–7
1. F, E, D, B, A, C
2. C
3. eavesdropping
4. A
5. the telephone
Chapters 8–9
6. lowers blood pressure, dilates blood vessels, keeps the heart from working too hard
7. She doesn't want Aunt Rebecca to get upset and have another spell.
8. "Charm is deceitful and beauty is vain, But a woman who fears the LORD, she shall be praised."

Page 87: Chapters 6–9:
Synonyms (circle all except the crossed-out words)
1. rude, ill-mannered, crude, mean, ~~polite,~~ discourteous, ~~boring~~
2. ~~relaxing~~, strenuous, tiring, ~~easy~~, difficult, ~~scenic~~, ~~refreshing~~
3. ~~whispering~~, pestering, tormenting, bothering, ~~giggling~~, ~~coughing~~, badgering
4. joined, met, ~~ran away from~~, gathered around, ~~irritated~~
5. enlarges, ~~contracts~~, ~~narrows~~, opens, widens, expands
6. bother, ~~calm~~, excite, stir up, irritate, ~~soothe~~, annoy
7. ~~glanced at~~, inspected, examined, ~~waved away~~, looked closely at
8. compressed, ~~opened~~, puckered, squeezed, ~~relaxed~~, tightened
9. ~~confused~~, firm, ~~worried~~, insistent, unyielding, unbendable
10. simple, rural, ~~advanced~~, backward, ~~up-to-date~~, ~~modern~~

Page 88: Geography: 1882
Railroad Routes to the West
Abilene: Daniel buys cowboy clothes
Denver: change trains NORTH
Cheyenne: change trains WEST
Ogden: stay on train WEST
Sacramento: change trains SOUTH
Fresno, California: ARRIVE!

Page 89: New York City
Bordering states (any order):
Vermont, Pennsylvania, New Jersey, Massachusetts, Connecticut
The five boroughs of New York City:

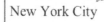

1. Manhattan
2. Brooklyn
3. Queens
4. The Bronx
5. Staten Island

New York City

Page 91: Chapters 10–13
Chapters 10–11
1. He whips the horse and races full speed toward town.
2. Daniel is abusing Pal, their horse, with the whip and reins.
3. False
4. Andi nearly loses her breakfast; the buggy's axle cracks; they have to walk to town; Andi receives cuts
5. He can read her facial expression; He sees her rumpled appearance
6. Cory Blake
7. They both attended Hoover Military Academy in the past.
8. Change clothes (or) get Shasta (or) go work with Riley.

Page 91: Chapters 10–13
Ch. 12 –13
9. Fighting Daniel
10. Daniel snooped and found her journal.
11. A couple of young cattle.
12. True
13. A

Page 97: Jesse James Crossword
ACROSS:
2. Ford
5. Abolitionist
6. Jesse
9. Quantrill
10. Frank
11. Alabama
12. Gallatin

DOWN:
1. Express
3. California
4. Missouri
7. Minnesota
8. Outlaw

Page 101: Word Search

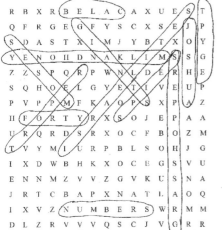

Page 92: Chapters 10–13
Vocabulary Matching
1. D
2. A
3. G
4. B
5. F
7. J
8. C
9. K
10. I
11. H

Digging Deeper:
Answers will vary.

Page 93: Character Clues:
1. Aunt Rebecca
2. Riley Prescott
3. Daniel Carter
4. Sid McCoy
5. Melinda
6. Chad
7. Andi
8. Sammy

Page 98: Chapters 14—17
Chapters 14 –15
1. B
2. **Circle**: Chad, Andi; **Box**: Mother, Justin
   Cross out: Mitch, Melinda, Lucy
3. robbed; beaten, left to die; shanghaied; murdered
4. no pay; live in the bunkhouse
5. Daniel hasn't pestered Andi. (or) Daniel seems to have made a turnaround in his behavior.
6. cockfighting (or) robbing stores

Chapters 16-17
7. Daniel is the thief.
8. burn down the barn
9. whiskey, tools, door-knockers, doorknobs, knives, tobacco tins, brooches, pendants
10. B
11. true
12. He wants the girls to ask Chad for money (a loan).
13. She thinks Daniel may have fallen down there.
14. Andi would never abandon her horse.

Page 99: Chapters 14–17 Vocabulary
1. success
2. searched
3. submissive
4. disgusting
5. guilt
6. take pleasure
7. hostility
8. get even
9. baby

Answer Key: *The Last Ride*- 4

Page 102: Chapters 18–21
Chapters 18-19
1. Andi is unconscious. (or) Andi is too sick to create an entry.
2. Justin, Chad, Mitch, Dr. Weaver
3. Mother: She is in Madera; Daniel: He went for help.
4. Cracked knee, dislocated shoulder, cracked ribs, concussion.
5. To not shoot Taffy.
6. Mitch
7. Andi is probably too weak to absorb this news; it's too hard of a blow to handle; she might get sicker; she might lose the will to live.

Chapters 20–21
8. They believe Daniel saved Andi's life by going for help.
9. She wants to go out to the barn (to see Taffy).
10. Chad
11. True
12. Daniel is in jail.
13. *A Journey to the Centre of the Earth*
14. Selfish, stubborn, unforgiving.
15. True

Page 103: Chapters 18–21:
Vocabulary
(other definitions possible)
1. deep cuts; scratches; gashes
2. unconsciousness
3. hot and airless
4. a litter for carrying someone
5. a hopeful outlook; confidence
6. Clasped; enclosed
7. kept; restrained
8. a bedpan; portable toilet
9. humiliating; embarrassing
10. hollered; yelled
11. dreadful; disgraceful
12. controlling; squashing
13. fascinated; charmed

Page 106: Five Elements of *The Last Ride* (Sample Answers)

CHARACTERS:

Andi Carter: almost 16; loves Taffy; wants to help manage the ranch   Chad: runs the ranch; Daniel Carter: almost-18 year old cousin from NYC; hates ranching; troublemaker; Riley Prescott: Circle C new wrangler; Elizabeth Carter: Andi's mother; Justin: Andi's oldest brother; married; has baby son, Sammy; Melinda & Mitch: Andi's siblings; Cory: Andi's friend

SETTING: Circle C ranch; spring & summer 1884

STORY PROBLEM: Andi has to learn to deal with a delinquent city cousin who endangers her life and the life of her mare, Taffy.

PLOT EVENTS (other answers are acceptable): Andi receives letter from NYC; Andi meets the new, young wrangler, Riley; Andi learns her colt Shasta will be trained by Riley; Andi learns Daniel is a troublemaker; Andi and Justin meet the train; Aunt Rebecca suffers from a weak heart; Andi must be considerate and do things she doesn't like to keep Rebecca from becoming ill; Daniel and Andi run the buggy into an orchard; Andi tries to teach Daniel lassoing and stall mucking; Daniel sneaks Andi's journal; Daniel disappears in San Francisco; Daniel steals from the town stores; Andi finds his cache; Andi is warned to keep quiet; Daniel causes Andi's accident; Taffy has to be put down; Andi is sick for a long time; Andi rejects her family when she learns of Taffy's death; Riley talks Andi into watching him work (end chapter 21)

STORY RESOLUTION: (answers will vary on how the student thinks Andi will resolve her problem)

Page 107 Chapters 22–26

Chapters 22–24

1. To take Andi with him to see the colts
2. By Andi's bitterness and unforgiveness, her family is sinking into gloom. (or) They are falling emotionally (in spirit).
3. B
4. Blows in her face; tosses his head; nickers; paws the ground
5. She feels guilty because Riley is right. She is hurting but she can't "let go."
6. Eight weeks (or) nine weeks
7. Andi rides Shasta for the first time with a saddle.
8. It's been so long since she's ridden. (or) She's not used to riding. (or) She hasn't ridden for over two months.

Chapters 25–26

9. Back to the gully where she fell and lost Taffy
10. It's time to stop running away. (or) It's time to face what happened and move on.
11. True
12. She can't mount Shasta because she's sore.
13. Midnight
14. It is very close to Andi's own experience.
15. She asks God to forgive her. She forgives brothers.
16. A birthday party.
17. She likes him.

Page 108: Ch. 22-26: Synonyms & Antonyms (synonym first; antonym)

1. prim & proper; casual
2. shut her mouth; talked a lot
3. gained; lost
4. bitterly; agreeably
5. sweet-talked; forced
6. clipped sounds; blurred sounds
7. unspoken; shouted
8. threateningly; encouragingly
9. disgraceful; honorable
10. criticized; praised
11. clowning; seriousness
12. determination; weakness

Page 111: New York City Travel Trivia

1. YES. St. Patrick's Cathedral opened in 1879; Catholic church
2. NO; Statue of Liberty opened in 1886; Construction began in 1875 (so Daniel could have seen it going up, but not visited.)
3. NO; Empire State Building opened in 1931; 102 stories
4. YES; Central Park established in 1857; False (it is the most-visited park in the U.S.)
5. NO; Flatiron Building opened in 1902; real name is Fuller Building; it looks like an iron.

Answer Key: *Courageous Love* – 1

Page 115 Chapters 1-5

Chapters 1–3

1. She's trick riding on Shasta.
2. Riley, he is teaching her and looking out for her.
3. It's too dangerous; her skirt can easily get caught; the falls are too bad.
4. A bloody nose; a cut over her eye
5. She has to go to Chad's engagement party tonight looking like this.
6. at college in Berkeley
7. It has been cut.
8. C
9. "For he shall give his angels charge over thee, to keep thee in all thy ways."

Chapters 4-5

10. Ellianna (Ellie) Coulter
11. Aunt Rebecca
12. She doesn't want to make a scene at Chad's party.
13. B
14. Cory confesses he cares about Andi in a deep way.
15. Johnny bumps her elbow and coffee splashes down her dress.
16. Glass breaks and something flies through the window.

Answer Key: *Courageous Love* – 2

Page 117: Trick Riding
1. Vaulting
2. Belly
3. Somersault
4. Crete
5. Standup
6. Roman riding
7. Strap
8. Tricks

Andi's favorite stunt:
The pickup trick

Page 121: Ch. 1-5 Vocabulary
1. B verb
2. A verb
3. B adjective
4. C verb
5. A verb
6. C noun
7. D adjective
8. B noun
9. C adjective

Page 122: Chapters 6–9
Chapters 6–7
1. A settee
2. Couch, sofa, or davenport
3. Aunt Rebecca's heart might act up at the terrible news.
4. Sid, Riley, Jem
5. Better check your heifers.
6. Answers will vary.
7. Levi

Chapters 8–9
8. False
9. Three
10. Alkali poisoning
11. Baking soda
12. →

Page 123: Vocabulary
1. D
2. B
3. I
4. H
5. C
6. G
7. F
8. E
9. J
10. A

Page 126: Barbed Wire Crossword Puzzle
ACROSS
2. barb
6. Glidden
7. two
8. Fresno
9. patent
10. cougar
11. trees

DOWN
1. cattle
3. fifty
4. respect
5. horses
6. gloves

Page 127: Chapters 10-13
Chapters 10-11
1. Mitch, Aunt Rebecca, Kate, Levi, Betsy, Hannah
2. The memory of the boundary dispute when the creek changed course.
3. (Answers will vary) dark scabs in the valley; trash—wheels, broken tools and plow; cracked pot, rags; crumbling outbuildings; dirty dishes; firewood scattered like jackstraws; children with stringy, matted hair; filthy faces
4. Fire
5. Riley
6. Her cousin Daniel
7. False

Chapters 12-13
8. sewing
9. She feels ill from the fire (coughing, etc.) but is healing.
10. false
11. Sky
12. San Quentin
13. They were on a stagecoach that Procopio held up eight years ago. They are upset he has escaped from prison.
14. Mateo Vega
15. Justin wants Andi to come and stay with Lucy while he is away in San Francisco.
16. Lucy is going to have a baby.

Page 128: Vocabulary
Meanings from Context (sentences will vary)
1. Resourcefulness
2. Dangers
3. Thrown-together
4. High-and-mighty
5. Feed
6. Stole
7. Fire
8. Energetic
9. Jumpy

Page 129: Character Clues
1. Sadie (Hollister)
2. Sid (McCoy)
3. Sammy
4. Kate (Katherine)
5. Andi
6. Sid (McCoy)
7. Diego
8. Riley (Prescott)
9. Procopio (Tomaso Rodendo)
10. Mitch

Favorite Character: Answers will vary.

Page 131: Where in the West?
Check to see that the states have been colored correctly. Use an atlas to check correct states' labeling.

Page 132: Chapters 14-17
Chapters 14-15
1. The kitchen is a disaster with spilled water and broken pottery.
2. Her locket
3. "Riley stood on the porch, hat in hand, <u>grinning like a possum</u>."
4. She shifts Sammy to cover her grease spot; she thinks she should have thought more about a tidy "me"; she crosses her arms over her soiled shirt; she wonders if he is blind.
5. Riley is grinning; he jumped at the chance to stop by; he misses working with Andi; Riley's face falls when he hears Justin may be gone a long time.
6. "You're as jumpy as a frog on a hot griddle."
7. The note that they are being watched.
8. A. Riley will drive them out to the ranch.
    B. Riley will stay the night with them.
Chapters 16-17
9. <u>Procopio (or Tomaso Redendo)</u>: handsome; mid forties; fancy suit; gold watch; clean, trimmed beard. <u>Vega</u>: scruffy; unwashed; unshaven; ill-fitting clothes
10. Jed Hatton
11. a derringer (pistol)
12. Procopio the bloodthirsty
13. The buggy goes into the river.

Page 133: Vocabulary
Words from Context
(accept anything close)
1. bounced up and down
2. angered or exasperated
3. a suit of clothes
4. peacefulness, calmness
5. feeling sick
6. a small traveling bag
7. an attacker
8. accomplice; partner; ally
9. obedience; submission
10. a thug; a bad guy
11. a crazy person; mentally ill
12. dropping; falling; plunging
13. a small pistol that holds only one shot.

Page 134: An Eye for an Eye
1. Matt. 5:38-39: "You have heard that it was said, 'An eye for an eye and a tooth for a tooth.' But I tell you not to resist an evil person. But whoever slaps you on your right cheek, turn the other to him also."
2. Rom. 12:19: "Beloved, do not avenge yourselves, but rather give place to wrath; for it is written, 'Vengeance is Mine, I will repay,' says the Lord."
3. The Law of Christ
4. Answers should speak to loving and forgiving others.
5. Ojo por ojo

Page 135:
Spanish
1. B
2. E
3. H
4. J
5. G
6. A
7. D
8. F
9. I
10. C

Page 136: Chapters 18-21
Chapters 18-19
1. Apúrate; vámonos
2. Jed Hatton
3. Sammy; Andi; Lucy
4. It's too dark to travel farther into the mountains.
5. "Jed prattled on like <u>the buzz of flies in Andi's ear.</u>"
6. B
7. near the north fork of the Kings River (or) the Sierras
Chapters 20-21
8. They are off on a raid and robbery of a local ranch.
9. There wasn't time. (The Spanish literally means "time failed us.")
10. She wants Lucy to have the saddled Dakota because it will be easier on her. Andi can ride bareback fine.
11. Three nights; three days
12. He gives Sammy to his wife to replace their dead son.
13. Santos
14. Gathering firewood
15. Tucker has followed Andi all the way to the camp.

Answer Key: *Courageous Love* – 4

Page 137: Circle Puzzle

1. turmoil
2. jubilant
3. comely
4. Kings
5. antagonize
6. ordeal
7. downcast
8. indigo
9. defiant
10. ransom
11. wily
12. falter
13. dallied
14. occupy

TUCKER AND RILEY

Page 139 : Who Am I?

1. Joaquin Murrieta
2. Tiburcio Vasquez
3. Procopio's father
4. Tomaso Procopio Rodendo
5. Rancher Pope

Page 140: Chapters 22-26

Chapters 22-24

1. Twelve days
2. *Be strong and of a good courage . . . for the Lord thy God is with thee.*
3. Riley has gone to Justin to ask permission to court Andi.
4. Ramón Ortega; Riley
5. He gives him gold from the Centerville Bank, which (he says) they robbed.
6. Chano Ortega; false
7. B
8. Jed Hatton
9. They ride Thunder out of the camp.

Chapters 25-26

10. She shot Vega.
11. C
12. She starts crying.
13. **Vega**: shot and wounded; **Benita**: Jed shot her, and she is wounded; **Procopio**: the posse shot him;
    Jed: has disappeared into the night.
14. June 12, 1886
15. Aunt Rebecca
16. She died last winter.
17. Andrea Grace Carter (or Gracie)

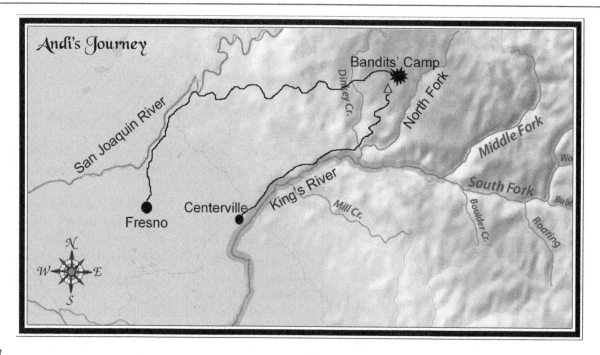

Made in the USA
Monee, IL
25 September 2020